FIVE-STAR
APPS

The best iPhone and iPad
apps for work and play

GLENN FLEISHMAN

Five-Star Apps: The best iPhone and iPad apps for work and play

Glenn Fleishman

Peachpit Press
1249 Eighth Street
Berkeley, CA 94710
510/524-2178
510/524-2221 (fax)

Find us on the Web at www.peachpit.com.
To report errors, please send a note to errata@peachpit.com.
Peachpit Press is a division of Pearson Education.

Editor: Clifford Colby
Production editor: Tracey Croom
Copyeditor: Charles Fleishman
Technical editor: Lex Friedman
Cover design: Aren Straiger
Interior design: Charlene Charles-Will

ISBN-13: 978-0-321-75143-0
ISBN-10: 0-321-75143-4

9 8 7 6 5 4 3 2 1

Printed and bound in the United States of America

For Ben, Lynn, & Rex
who make a house a home

Table of Contents

Introduction

What makes a five-star app? A program has to be interesting, even if the task it's performing is routine. When you look at a dozen apps that have the same informational, utilitarian, or entertainment goal, five-star apps have that extra something special that floats to the top.

In reading thousands of recommendations, testing hundreds of apps, and then choosing the set that appears in this book, I found that the best apps were ones that surprised me and charmed me, even for ordinary tasks.

A good example is Ocarina, an early iPhone app that continues to be a bestseller more than two years after the introduction of the App Store.

Anyone could have come up with a pedestrian ocarina program, in which you blow into the microphone to simulate breath going into the ancient musical instrument with onscreen buttons controlling finger positions.

What Ge Wang and his Smule team brought to Ocarina was depth, discovery, charm, and a community. The more you use Ocarina, the better you can become at it. Dig at the program and you can set a different key or musical mode. Tap a global icon and see—and hear!—other people playing the program worldwide. Go online and find transcribed scores in Ocarina notation to play yourself.

It's not just an app; it's a small universe.

Not every app is Ocarina, but every program in this book has some combination of stellar qualities: a high degree of finish (interface, graphics, and program action), utility (at a task, at having fun, at facilitating creativity or learning), and persistence.

That last point is a key one. For five-star apps, the developer keeps tweaking and updating the program to add more features and fix things that aren't right, He or she tries to bring to the app more of what existing users want, and what might make the program more appealing to new users.

The other aspect of my personal five-star apps is that they rarely average more than 3½ to 4 stars on Apple's App Store rating system. That struck me as odd when I started researching the book. Fabulous programs—universally well reviewed by magazines and Web sites, with great word of mouth, and which tested well for me—had a lot of "meh" in the reviews.

That's partly the vagary of reviewers and partly an outcome of Apple's review system. Five stars may seem like too many; three or four fairer. And, before iOS 4, Apple asked for ratings whenever an app was deleted, hardly a great time to get an opinion. It was also easy to mistap and rate an app with a single star. Reviewers also complain after purchase about the cost of apps. I used quality, not price, as a factor in picking app.

For this book, five stars are what I give all the apps in it using my own personal rating system. I hope you'll agree—and tell me about your own five-star apps.

Glenn Fleishman
Seattle, Washington

MORE: At the bottom of many reviews, you can find information about other versions of the app or related apps, as well as details about whether or not an account on a Web site is required to use the app effectively.

Using Apps in iOS

While using an iPhone, iPad, or iPod touch is a thing of simplicity not to be rivaled in the history of mankind— where's the mild sarcasm font?—it's helpful to know some background information about apps in particular and iOS in general. Which apps work on which devices? What's this Game Center app that's on my home screen? How do I move files back and forth to a computer? And more. Read on!

What's iOS?

iOS is the operating system that handles all of the interaction and hardware control on an iPhone, iPad, and iPod touch. iOS was called iPhone OS for some time before the iPad was released, even though it worked on the iPod touch as well.

Apple decided to avoid confusion by shortening the name. iOS isn't an abbreviation for anything; it's just marketing.

At this writing iOS 4.2 is just being released for all three kinds of devices.

Compatibility

Not all apps run the same way on all iOS devices. Apps have one of three kinds of compatibility, which is listed in the iTunes Store for every program.

Open **http://5str.us/vwx**, for instance, and look below the price, release date, and other information. You'll see a block of text that starts with "Requirements."

> Requirements:Compatible with iPhone and iPod touch (4th generation). Requires iOS 3.1 or later.

This text is a little confusing, because Apple uses so many different versions of it. You can rely on the description to tell you whether or not an app will work on a given iOS device, and the minimum version of iOS required.

I made sure every app in this book works with iOS 4. Some apps may not launch on versions earlier than iOS 4 because of special features required to make the program work.

I use a pair of icons in the book to show this compatibility at a glance. The left member is larger than its partner to the right. The left icon represents an iPad; the littler one, an iPhone and iPod touch. I mark icons **red** for not compatible, **green** for apps designed for a given device, and blue for compatible in a special mode. Let's look at each further:

Compatible with iPhone, iPod touch, and iPad: These apps are designed for the iPhone/iPod touch screen size, but will work in a special mode on the iPad. The app's screen is centered on an iPad at its iPhone/iPod touch size, but a tap of a 2x button in the corner doubles the size in both dimensions. It's not ideal, as most graphics become pixillated, and taps aren't captured perfectly in games.

TIP: I'll also include advice about using an app well, such as special hidden modes, tricks to avoid wasting time, or fun trivia about the app.

Compatible with iPad: Such apps are designed for the iPad, and cannot be installed on an iPhone or iPad touch. Many apps, especially games, come in two versions: one designed for the iPhone/iPod touch and the other an iPad-only version, often with "HD" in its name. This compatibility type is often described as "iPad only."

"This app is designed for both iPhone and iPad": A program that takes advantage of both sized displays, showing an interface and graphics appropriate to the device on which it's installed. Despite saying "iPhone," such apps also work on the iPod touch. This kind of compatibility is often called "universal." In the iTunes Store, on the app's detail page, a ▣ (plus sign) appears next to the price and an additional label appears below the price as well as the "requirements" information even further below.

In some cases, apps have even stricter requirements. Some programs will only run if the device has a camera built in, which means an iPhone or a 4th-generation iPod touch. And some of those apps can't work with an iPhone older than the 3GS (2009) model. A few flashlight programs rely on the LED flash that's only found in the iPhone 4 at this writing.

Other apps need a fast processor to carry out their tasks, which means an iPad, iPhone 4, or 4th-generation iPod touch. These requirements are often noted in small type.

I call out exceptions to the compatibility guidelines for each app as applicable.

Links & Prices

Next to every app's name in the book, as well as in notes and elsewhere, you will see links that look like:

http://5str.us/x2m

These links are shortcuts that I set up to take you straight to the destination, whether it's an app or a search result on the iTunes Store, or a link elsewhere.

Prices are listed with every app, but my experience is that they change constantly for sales and competition.

Background

iOS 4 added the capability for apps to keep running in a limited fashion when you switched to another program, answered a phone call, or pressed the home button.

The three main kinds of app-related tasks that can be performed in the background are:

Audio: A music, podcast, or other audio playback program can continue to play audio.

Location: GPS navigators and other apps can continue to update your location in their internal map even though they can't display the current position. Voice navigation can continue, however, and push notifications if a phone call is un.

VoIP: An in-progress Internet telephone call can continue uninterrupted, and you can receive calls even when the app isn't in the foreground, or your device's screen is locked. This includes Skype (p. 106) and Line2 (p. 107).

For apps that offer audio, navigation, and VoIP, I explain the specific background features supported.

Only iOS devices released starting in 2009 can let apps use background tasks. That's the iPhone 3GS and 4, the 3rd- and 4th-generation iPod touch, and all iPad models.

Game Center

Game Center for iOS 4.1 appeared as this book was in preparation, and many of the games and other programs involving buddy lists still needed to be updated to support the new feature when we went to press.

Game Center hooks you up with your friends. It's a social network, but unfortunately not linked into Facebook, Twitter, or even Apple's Ping as I write this. And you can't search for friends; you have to ask them for their handles. These aspects need improvement.

But Game Center is a nifty way to compare scores on leaderboards, and play live multiplayer games over the Internet. I expect that we'll see thousands of games link in to Game Center, because it allows developers to avoid having to build their own networks for games.

For games that have components in desktop Mac and Windows software, on Web sites, and via other mobile platforms, you might see a Game Center option and a tie-in to these programs' own networks, too.

Installing Apps

You have two ways to add apps to an iOS device: through iTunes and through the App Store program on the device.

In either case, you need an iTunes Store account, which was also required when you set up your iOS device. However, you can create a new account for purposes of purchasing and syncing. The iTunes account needs to have a payment method associated with it, too.

The App Store lists each program's price and download size. Some programs are tiny, under a few megabytes; others may be as big as 2 gigabytes (GB), like navigation software.

Apple only lets you download apps up to 20 megabytes (MB) in size over a 3G network. However, those sub-20 MB chunks add up. If you have a limited data plan (200 MB), you may want to avoid app downloads except while connected to a Wi-Fi network.

With every review or software reference in the book, this book lists a short URL. You can type in that URL and be redirected to the app in question without going through additional steps. You can also go to **http://5str.us/** and enter the short code for the same result. The links launch iTunes in Mac OS X or Windows, or the App Store app when using iOS's Mobile Safari.

TIP: You can invite friends to a game, but you don't have to sit and wait for them to join. After sending the invitation, you can exit the app. If your friend later accepts, a notification appears to let you relaunch the game and start to play.

In-app purchases are add-ons for a program that you buy after installing the software. These purchases are sometimes available within settings; other times, a popup window suggests you buy something! Add-ons can include rocket ships for games, subscriptions for services, or a fee to remove advertising, depending on the software. Your iTunes Store account is used for these purchases.

iTunes on the Desktop

You must pick a single computer to which you synchronize your apps, movies, music, and other media. That copy of iTunes is where you will make your app purchases. It's also where apps are copied the next time you sync following the purchase of programs on an iPhone, iPad, or iPod touch.

You can buy or obtain free apps by launching iTunes with or without an iOS device plugged in. Click the iTunes Store item in the left sidebar under the Store label. You can use the search field in the upper-right corner to find apps by name, or browse by category, featured, and best-selling programs.

To buy an app with a fee attached or download a free app, click the price or the Free App label. If you haven't recently logged in to iTunes, the program prompts you for your password.

The app is downloaded into a folder on your computer, and is now available to sync with any iOS device linked to the same iTunes Store account on that computer. (An unlimited number of iOS devices may link to the same account.)

You can set your iOS device to add any new software you purchase, although

that can get out of hand if you buy a lot of apps. (My library now contains hundreds of apps, and I don't want them on every device I own.)

Or, you can select individual apps and add them to a given device's app line-up. iTunes also lets you rearrange apps on home screens, organize them into folders, and move files back and forth for certain apps (see iTunes File Sharing.)

With a device plugged in, select it by name in the left sidebar under Devices. Then click the Apps tab in the main iTunes window. With Sync Apps checked at the top, you can check or uncheck Automatically Sync New Apps to control that behavior.

With that new apps sync box unchecked, check the box next to an app in the list to add it to the device; or uncheck the box to remove it. You can also drag apps around the screens, drag apps off the screen, or drag apps into a screen.

Click Sync at the end to match everything up.

App Store App

Instead of using iTunes on a computer, you can use the App Store app—preinstalled on every iOS device—to purchase software so long as you are connected to an active network.

You can follow a link in Mobile Safari, or launch the app directly. Tap App Store's Search tab, and type in the name of a program you want. Select the app, and tap the Free or price button to obtain it; the button changes to Install, which you tap again to complete the transaction. iOS prompts you to enter your iTunes Store password.

The app will now start to download if you're on Wi-Fi, or if it's under 20 MB and you're connected to 3G on an iPhone or 3G iPad. (You can still buy larger apps over 3G, but downloads won't start until you're next connected to Wi-Fi.)

Warning! After you enter your iTunes Store password, your iOS device remains logged in for several minutes. This can be a problem if you hand your phone off to someone else, like a child, who then proceeds without malice to make in-app purchases. Online forums are rife with complaints about "free" apps that have in-app purchases for add-on packs.

You can log out to prevent these purchases. The setting is a bit hidden. From the Featured tab, scroll way down to the bottom, where you find the Account button. Tap that button, and tap Sign Out.

Finding Settings

App settings can be located in one of two main places, but are sometimes hidden elsewhere. This can be frustrating.

Within the app. Many apps that have options to set (such as entering a user name and password, or toggling on and off background music) use a gear icon to provide access. Tap the gear, and then change settings.

In the Settings app. Launch the Settings app, and swipe downwards. There, you'll find all the apps that choose to depend on the Settings app for configuration options. Tap on an app's name to make changes.

Unfortunately, many apps have options both within themselves and in the Settings app. (The Settings app in some of these cases contains just an app reset or debugging switch, however.)

Elsewhere. Some apps also hide settings elsewhere, such as an Options button or other label when you're starting a game or adding an item to a list.

iTunes File Sharing

iTunes is more than just a conduit for syncing apps and media with an iOS device: it can also let you manage which files are associated with apps like GoodReader, Air Sharing, ComicZeal, and many others.

To add, remove, or download files this way, follow these steps:

1. Connect your mobile device to a computer with iTunes.

2. Launch or switch to iTunes.

TIP: You can also use Settings > General > Restrictions to set a code to prevent use of certain iOS features, including denying in-app purchases.

File Sharing

The applications listed below can transfer documents between your iPad and this computer.

Apps	GoodReader Documents		
Air Sharing	2010_branch_hours.pdf	5/5/10 9:26 PM	80 KB
ArtStudio	books.google.com.html	4/3/10 10:16 PM	40 KB
ComicZeal4	Car Rental LAX Mideway.pdf	7/12/10 9:06 PM	168 KB
Corkulous	Daddy_Long_Legs.pdf	5/6/10 9:16 PM	2.3 MB
	DSC_0131.tif	4/3/10 2:31 PM	17.3 MB
Crosswords	DSC_0530 2.jpg	5/5/10 9:24 PM	3.1 MB
DocsToGo	DSC_0530.jpg	5/5/10 9:24 PM	3.1 MB
	Howards_End.pdf	4/3/10 10:17 PM	5.8 MB
GoodReader	Mathboard	9/26/10 8:45 PM	440 KB
	Picture 2.jpg	5/6/10 9:17 PM	144 KB
Google Earth	Picture 3.jpg	9/24/10 10:24 PM	720 KB
	Picture.jpg	4/3/10 10:19 PM	128 KB
	PSG11_CUG_EN_03.pdf	4/3/10 2:31 PM	5.7 MB

Add...   Save to...

3. Select your device from the Devices list in iTunes in the sidebar.

4. Click the Apps tab at top.

5. Scroll down within the tab to File Sharing.

At left, the Apps list displays any programs that can have files moved in and out in this way. Select an app and the Documents list at right shows everything stored with that program.

- Click Add to select files from a selection dialog box. You can also drag files from the desktop into the Documents list.

- Select a file or folder and press Delete to remove items.

- Select a file or folder and click Save To to make a copy on your hard drive.

Unfortunately, you can't navigate down through folders in the list to retrieve, add, or delete items within them.

WebDAV File Sharing

Several apps use WebDAV to allow access to files and folders by other computers and devices connected to the same network. Mac OS X and Windows have built-in WebDAV access.

WebDAV works over a local network to other computers connected to the same network. That means that your iOS device has to be connected via Wi-Fi to a network, and any computer that wants to access the device has to be connected via Wi-Fi or Ethernet to the same network. WebDAV doesn't allow your iOS device to share its files over 3G.

To use WebDAV, first start the file-sharing software on your iOS device in whatever app you're using. Some apps keep WebDAV active for as long as the program is in the foreground, like Air Sharing Pro. Others, like GoodReader, require that you tap a button to start WebDAV service.

The app should show you a numeric address or other name by which you can access your iOS device. The number is typically in the form **10.0.1.25:8080**. You'll need that number.

WebDAV servers only run as long as the program is active. For some apps, you tap Close or exit a pop-up or popover menu, and that halts the WebDAV server. With other apps, exiting the program turns off the server.

In any of those cases, however, that causes the shared information to becomes immediately unavailable. It's best to unmount a volume from a Mac or make sure all file transfers are completed under Windows before turning off the WebDAV server.

Here's how to connect to your device from Mac OS X and Windows.

From a Mac:

1. In the Finder, select Go > Connect to Server (Command-K). Enter the address in the form:

   http://10.0.1.10:8080

   substituting whatever address the app provides. (The dot and extra number mark a "port," which lets multiple servers work on the device at once.)

2. Click OK.

3. You should be prompted to enter a username and password. If you set one in the app, enter that information; otherwise, just click OK.

The app's shared files show up just like another hard drive on your Desktop. Double-click to open the drive. You should be able to copy files to and from the drive and delete files.

To unmount the drive from your Desktop, first select it, and then choose the File menu's Eject item.

From Windows (XP, Vista, and 7).

Follow these steps to mount a WebDAV server for file access.

1. Right-click the Computer icon on your desktop, and select Map Network Drive. (If the computer icon isn't on your desktop, right-click the Windows button at the lower left and select Windows Explorer.)

2. Click the link at the bottom, "Connect to a Web site that you can use to store your documents and pictures." The Add Network Location wizard launches.

3. Click Next.

4. Click Choose a Custom Network Location, then click Next.

5. Enter the address of the app's WebDAV server, such as

   http://10.0.1.25:8080

   and click Next. You may need to wait a moment for the next step to finish.

6. Type a name that identifies the app's server, such as **iPad server**. Click Next.

7. Click Finish.

A window will open on the desktop with the share which works just like any hard drive.

Windows isn't as concerned about unmounting WebDAV volumes, and there's no way to eject or disconnect a mounted volume. Just make sure you don't open a file directly from the server's folder; copy it to your computer first.

iOS Supported File Formats

iOS has a long list of image, audio, document, and video file formats that it can read natively—the operating system has all the built-in support to display or play the files in the way they were intended.

Any app that's written to display documents or images or play back media can use any of those types with no extra work by the programmer.

Supported formats include popular formats such as PDF and Microsoft Word, but also a number of more obscurely named audio and video standards.

It's quite hard to know from looking at a media file you want to access—its extension or other details—whether or not it will work under iOS. In the Video section of the book, I review two apps that are designed to convert and play back just about any kind of audio and video file to get around this limitation.

You can find a full list of the file types that iOS supports at **http://5str.us/ppm**; read the text under TV and Video and Audio Playback.

Acknowledgements

I could not have written and produced this book without the help and encouragement of many others.

My father, Charles Fleishman, was my primary copyeditor, and acted as sense checker: he's a relatively new iPhone 4 owner and long-time Mac user. Lex Friedman, who I met via Twitter through colleagues, provided exceptional last-stage editing and technical review.

My wife, Lynn Warner, gave me critical feedback in planning the book and read for sense. My children, Ben and Rex, who you will see in photos throughout this title, coped with me being less available for extended periods during part of the book's creation—because I promised them they would appear in photos throughout the book.

In my shared office, long-time colleague Jeff Carlson (himself finishing two books at the same time to my one) was a touchstone for sanity and humor. Old friend David Blatner helped me put InDesign CS5 in its place.

At Peachpit, Tracey Croom kept production moving smoothly, while editor Cliff Colby was a specialist in the soothing and encouraging phone call.

My thanks, also, to the hundreds of people who suggested apps for the book and took the time to explain why they liked a given program.

This book was produced under the influence of Glenn Gould, The Police, and They Might Be Giants.

I love to hear from readers. You can email me at **glenn@5str.us** or follow me on twitter **@glennf**.

1

Reading

The iPad was designed for reading books and other long-form material. The Retina Display in the iPhone 4 and 4th-generation iPod touch likewise ache to display words. In this chapter, see the best apps for reading books, newsfeeds, documents, and comics.

BOOKS / NEWSFEEDS / REMEMBERING / DOCUMENTS / COMICS

iBooks

FREE* • Apple • http://5str.us/8yw

Read and buy ebooks and read PDFs with a booky feel

iBooks is Apple's entry into the some-what crowded ebook reader app market. Designed first for the iPad, and then brought over to the iPhone and iPod touch, iBooks tries to capture the nature of books while making it easy to scan through pages, bookmark, make notes, and search.

You acquire books in one of three ways. First up is Apple's online iBookstore, still rather modest at this writing compared to those offered by Amazon and Barnes & Noble. Apple includes free books from Project Gutenberg and other sources, as well as commercial fiction and nonfiction. (The iBookstore is reachable only through an iOS device.)

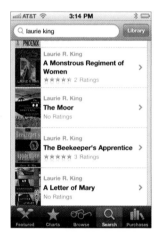

Unprotected EPUB files can be imported, too; EPUB is a publishing-industry standard for producing books that can have fonts and formatting resized without losing images attached to various parts of the book. EPUB files have to be copied to iBooks via iTunes (see p. xv) instead of opened in iOS.

Finally, iBooks can also store and read PDF files, which can be copied over from many apps (through the Open With option), or managed via iTunes. There are better PDF readers than iBooks (such as GoodReader and Air Sharing), but iBooks does a perfectly good job.

Books and PDFs appear in a faux bookshelf; the Books/PDFs tabs appear only if you have PDFs loaded. Tap a book to open it. (If you don't see a book you've purchased or obtained at no cost from the iBooks store, tap the Store button, and then tap the Purchases icon at lower right to download missing items.)

ACCOUNT: *You need a free iTunes Store account to make purchases or download free books from the iBooks store, as well as to sync book items among multiple devices.

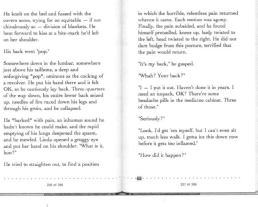

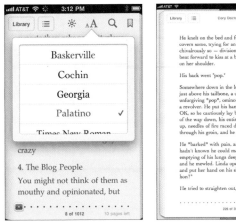

You can opt to read in either portrait or landscape orientation, and the book reflows for direction. On an iPad, the landscape view breaks a book into two side-by-side pages.

iBooks lets you change attributes of the page, such as the typeface and size.

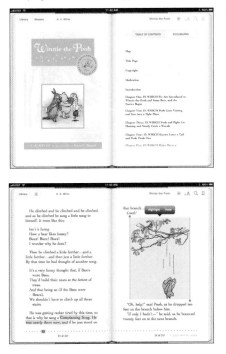

You can also adjust brightness directly in the app, bookmark pages for later reference, highlight ranges of text and images, and leave notes in the text.

Books can be searched for keywords; the same pane that shows the results lets you jump to perform a query at Google and Wikipedia for the same words in Mobile Safari.

Your iTunes Store account is used to manage ownership for books you purchase, but it also handles syncing notes, bookmarks, and highlights across all your iOS devices with the same account.

OH, BOTHER: Winnie The Pooh is a free download with iBooks. The connection? Winnie the Pooh copyrights are owned by Disney. Disney's biggest shareholder is Apple CEO and co-founder Steve Jobs. Hurray for Pooh!

Barnes & Noble Nook

FREE • Barnes & Noble • http://5str.us/bh4

This reading app offers superior control over type and page display

Nook, a mid-2010 replacement for Barnes & Noble's previous Reader program, has style and panache. It's now among the best book-reading programs. Nook offers the most extensive control over display, even allowing you to set an inset margin.

Like all iOS reading programs except Apple's iBooks, Nook doesn't let you shop for reading material within the app; you must use Mobile Safari to make purchases. Nook has access to a large library of both free and paid books.

Once you purchase items, they appear on Nook's main page. Books that aren't stored on the device you're using have a Download label at the bottom; tap, and the work is retrieved along with the last-read position in the book.

Pages can be read in portrait or landscape orientation, but the same settings aren't necessarily best for each view.

DRACULA (BARNES & NOBLE CLASSICS SERIES)

CHAPTER XXIV

DR SEWARD'S PHONOGRAPH DIARY, SPOKEN BY VAN HELSING

This to Jonathan Harker.

You are to stay with your dear Madam Mina. We shall go to make our search—if I can call it so, for it is not search but

I use the various options for changing font, color, size, line spacing, and margin to create custom themes, making one appropriate for wide reading in landscape and the other for narrow reading in portrait.

The version of the app tested lacks annotation, highlight, and bookmark syncing between the Nook hardware and desktop software. But its better qualities make up for that lack—and I expect those features to come, perhaps by the time you're reading this review.

MORE: An iPad-only version is also available (free, **http://5str.us/kme**).

Kindle ▮▮

FREE • Amazon.com • http://5str.us/fmi

Premier ebook reader offers access to an ocean of ancient, recent, modern books

Why buy a book you can read in only one place? Amazon's answer is: you shouldn't. The Kindle app is part of an ecosystem. Amazon makes the hundreds of thousands of books you can buy or get for free from its Kindle Store available to the iOS app, as well as to Kindle hardware (the smaller-sized Kindle and larger Kindle DX), and apps for other mobile devices and desktops.

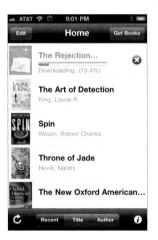

Because of limits Apple imposes on how items are sold within apps, you are directed to Amazon's Web site to purchase books or load free books. You can *send* these to specific Kindle apps or hardware; the next time you launch Kindle on an iPhone or other iOS device the book immediately starts downloading.

Reading is a pleasure in the Kindle app, which lets you pick among some presets for the typeface, font size, and background color. Page flipping is as simple as tapping. You also tap to leave notes or create a bookmark for future reference. The app continuously registers your current reading position and syncs notes and bookmarks with Amazon's central servers. This allows you to pick up where you left off in any other Kindle app or device.

TIP: Tap the i icon in the lower right and flip Popular Highlights to On, and you can see what other people using Kindle are highlighting in their copies of the same book. This is both interesting and annoying.

Reeder ■■

$2.99* • Silvio Rizzi • http://5str.us/i22

Distraction-free presentation and easy forwarding of feed items

Reeder is a straightforward interface for accessing the RSS feeds and other news you've subscribed to via Google Reader (http://5str.us/p72). Google Reader acts as a central synchronized repository for Reeder and other desktop and mobile newsreader programs.

While there are other apps covered in this chapter that reformat RSS news-feeds into something richer, there's also a place for those who want a tool that presents that information in the most straightforward way. That's Reeder.

Reeder pulls down updates from Google Reader on request. The main inter-face uses a star, a circle, and a set of three horizontal lines to indicate items marked as favorites, unread items, and all items or feeds.

I typically find myself in the "circle" mode, tapping the Unread link at the top. This shows me feeds in the order of mostly recently received first (indicated by a clock icon at lower right). Tap the feed (signal waves) icon to show unread items divvied up by feed instead.

Reeder's strength, beyond simplicity, is in how well it shares what you're read-ing. You can share, transfer, or post to services or programs like Instapaper, Mobile Safari, Delicious, Twitter, email, and many more. (Active services can be set via the Settings app.)

Reeder works only over Wi-Fi when installed unless you change an option in Settings > Reeder.

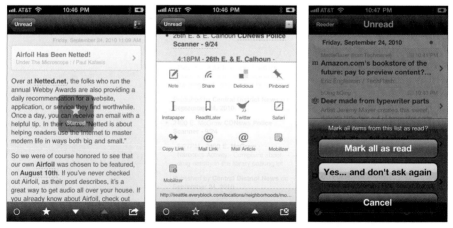

MORE: Reeder is also available in an iPad edition with a view where items are represented as stacks of paper ($4.99, **http://5str.us/wt7**). **ACCOUNT:** *Free Google Reader account required.

I Instapaper ■▪

$4.99* • Marco Arment • http://5str.us/mt2

Don't despair when you can't read a Web page right now. Read it later

Instapaper answers the question of what to do when you find something on the Web that you want to remember and read later. If I immediately read everything I was interested in that was forwarded to me, I would never have had the time to write this book.

Bookmarks were once the answer, and those of you with 100 bookmarks or more that you never consult, raise your hand? (I'm raising mine.)

Instapaper works on the Web, whether in a desktop browser or Mobile Safari, by giving you a Read Later bookmark. After creating and logging into a free account at Instapaper, you install this link, and you're ready to start saving links. (The Mobile Safari installation is a little involved, but the documentation walks you through step by step.)

Whenever you're on a Web page and tap or click Read Later, a little behind-the-scenes JavaScript copies the URL to your Instapaper account. The text of the page in a stripped-down format is also stored for later viewing.

Launch the Instapaper app and, with your account information in place, all the articles and pages you've marked for reading later are synchronized along with any folders you've made for orga-nizing pages.

When you select an item to read, you're shown the reduced formatting first—it's stored on your device. This lets you read articles and other Web pages while

away from a network. Tap the arrow-in-a-rectangle button at lower right, and you can archive the item, move it to a folder, and share it through many means (email, Tweeting, and so on). You can also open the item in an in-app Web browser to see the full original HTML glory of the page you marked to read.

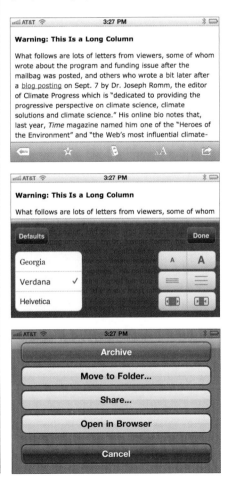

Flipboard ■■

FREE • Flipboard • http://5str.us/j86

Presentation of feeds, Twitter, Facebook, and more in a magazine-like format

Flipboard takes a small number of interesting, regularly updated data sources, and presents the results like a magazine. The app takes the links, photos, and videos of an RSS, Twitter, or Facebook feed, and presents them in a way that you can't believe was generated entirely without a human being handling the layout. It's an automatic periodical.

You can add prefabricated feeds from the list offered by Flipboard, including a variety of news, independent, and photo sites. You can add feeds from Twitter (by name and list) and your Facebook feed.

Each time you launch the app, a "cover" image drawn from a feed fills the screen; these rotate through almost like a slideshow if you don't move on. Swipe (or "flip") from the right edge to the left, and the table of contents appears with nine squares per page. (Swipe left to add items to more pages.) Each item in the contents shows an appropriate image, again drawn from the newsfeed.

Tap a square, and the RSS items, tweets, or Facebook updates are shown at varying sizes, depending on length and context. Photos and videos are extracted from links, and typically shown large. Articles linked or in the RSS feed are previewed. Tap on any item and get more of it, often with a link to load the Web page (within the app).

Flipboard transforms the stream of undifferentiated updates we receive into something beautiful, comprehensible, and compact. It's digestible without losing the flavor. It would be nice to add any RSS or newsfeed, but there is a benefit to the simplicity of choice, too. Flipboard isn't a newsreader; it's a medium.

Times for iPad

$7.99 • Acrylic Software • http://5str.us/zm4

A new kind of RSS reader presents feeds as an ersatz newspaper

Times makes newspapers out of RSS feeds, even feeds from newspapers. Traditional RSS readers—if traditional makes sense for a newish technology—organize the items that come from feeds as headlines, in most cases making items appear like email subject lines.

Times has a radically different approach. Why not make news look like news? While the app comes with prefab feeds—so that you're not looking at a blank page—you can add feeds from any site you want. (There's no discovery process to find feeds at this writing, but that's a minor cavil.)

Feeds appear as columns, which you can make wider or narrower. The items in feeds, including images, can be displayed as a series of headlines, as a series of images, or various combinations from a set of layout options. The app comes with a few categories defined at the top, like Technology and Science, but it's easy enough to change those or add your own.

You can scroll up and down in columns, as well as drag left and right to see more columns. Tap an item, and it opens in a rolldown frame, approximating a newspaper page.

In landscape view, items may be added to a shelf that can be revealed at the top of the virtual page as a kind of bookmark. You can also choose to view items in an in-app browser. Items can be shared via email, Twitter, and Facebook.

Times re-envisions the flow of information coming from feeds all over the Web into something comprehensible and attractive.

TIP: You can make a section wider than the screen width and then swipe right to see more columns of feeds.

GoodReader for iPad ▪▪

$0.99 • Good.iWare • http://5str.us/jl7

Need to retrieve a file from somewhere else, store it, and read it?

GoodReader is the missing link in iOS file transfer and management. An iOS device can view attachments in email, or view many file formats linked on a Web page using Mobile Safari. But iOS by itself neither lets you store documents in a common location nor retrieve files from Internet file-storage services. GoodReader adds all that and more.

On the incoming side, GoodReader can connect with many Internet storage services using the WebDAV standard. It has special entries for Dropbox and MobileMe iDisk, as well as prefab settings for several other service providers. Pictures from the Photo Library can also be added. Any file you retrieve is stored locally, but not automatically updated if the remote copy changes.

Three in-app purchases, each 99 cents, let you add file-retrieval options: email (retrieve messages or attachments), FTP (both regular and Secure FTP), and Google Docs. (The same is true for the iPhone/iPod version of GoodReader.)

Files can be added via iTunes File Sharing (see p. xv). You can opt to move files around over a network, too: GoodReader has a built-in WebDAV server that allows remote access on the same Wi-Fi network from Mac OS X, Windows, and apps running on other iOS devices—including GoodReader.

The WebDAV server lets you copy, delete, rename, and add files to GoodReader's file storage. (For more about using WebDAV, see p. xvi.) The WebDAV server can be set up so that when someone tries to access files, you're prompted to accept or reject. (I like the enthuastic **!!!** after Yes.)

MORE: GoodReader also comes in two iPhone/iPod touch versions: GoodReader for iPhone ($0.99, **http://5str. us/ryi**) and GoodReader Lite for iPhone (free, **http://5str.us/gjx**). The Lite version stores just five documents.

GoodReader shines at handling PDFs, far better than iOS's built-in capability. GoodReader includes zone-based navigation, where tapping in different areas lets you move forward and backward or trigger other activities.

PDFs can be searched, and bookmarks and the table of contents used for navigation. You can view annotations made in Acrobat or elsewhere, and attach notes to PDF pages. A PDF Reflow option extracts the text of a PDF one page at a time for easier onscreen reading. You can also copy the text and email it.

The Manage Files feature lets you mark files once they're stored in GoodReader, You can mark a file as a favorite, open a document in another app, rename a file, or create a compressed ZIP archive of selected items.

On the reading side, GoodReader can handle all the formats built into iOS (see complete list on p. xviii), including playing back supported audio and video.

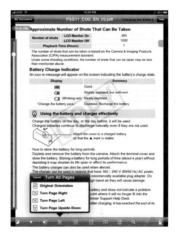

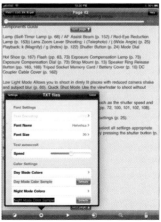

Air Sharing Pro ▪▪

$6.99 • Avatron Software • http://5str.us/px5

Store, view, retrieve, delete, print, and email files remotely or on an iOS device

The problem with mobility is that the file you need is always somewhere else. Air Sharing Pro eliminates that issue, and offers quite a bit more, too. The program has three distinct elements, and each can be highly useful.

First, it retrieves files from wherever you've put them. The app offers built-in support to access a variety of remote file servers and storage systems. This includes MobileMe iDisk and Dropbox, any server using the WebDAV protocol for file access, and Secure FTP. By

entering email account login information, the program can pull down attachments from mail messages. Air Sharing can also use Bonjour networking to find WebDAV servers on the same Wi-Fi network as your device.

Second, you can view or copy a file from any directory or folder you bring up. PDF files may be searched, and the app lets you use PDF thumbnails, bookmarks, and table of contents entries to navigate.

Files can also be sent to printers over Wi-Fi. The printers have to offer Bonjour network discovery, which most modern units have. The print option appears when you tap the action button at the lower left of a document. Available printers are listed. Once you select a printer, you can choose a page range, and paper type, as well as modify printer-specific options such as paper feed and paper type.

MORE: Air Sharing ($2.99, **http://5str.us/xch**) has a $3.99 in-app purchase to upgrade to full Air Sharing Pro features. There's also an iPad version called Air Sharing HD ($9.99, iPad only, **http://5str.us/d7d**).

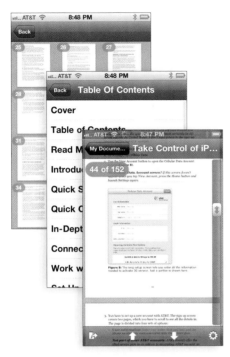

Air Sharing also sports a number of file-handling tools in any document view. Tap Edit, then select files, and tap the gear icon in the lower right. The app can then compress the files into a ZIP archive, rename them, or delete them. But it can also copy files. If you choose copy, an icon with a paperclip is shown at the upper right. Navigate to any other server or the My Documents folder, and you can copy files to that location. You can also move files, which deletes after copy.

Avatron has a less-featured version of Air Sharing that costs $4 less: it omits WebDAV, printing, file, and advanced PDF viewing features, but can be upgraded in-app to the full Pro version. (Avatron has a comparison chart: **http://5str.us/pk9**.)

Third, and finally, Air Sharing Pro has a built-in file server. That's right: your iOS device can show up on a local Wi-Fi network as a server that you or others can use (with optional password protection and encryption) to retrieve, add, or exchange files.

Documents To Go Premium ▮▮

$16.99 • DataViz • http://5str.us/19b

Edit your Office documents wherever they live

To make an iOS device work for a business professional, it needs to be able to handle the formats for the universally employed word processing, spreadsheet, and presentation programs from Microsoft—the power trio of Word, Excel, and PowerPoint.

While any iOS app that views files can show you the contents of those formats, few can make any changes to them or create new files in those formats. That's where Documents To Go Premium (Office Suite) comes in.

The app can create and edit any of those formatted files, as well as view all other native iOS formats (see p. xviii). It works on the small screen or the iPad, and is best used with an external keyboard for extended editing or writing.

Select a document from any of the file location tabs, like Local, and it opens in an editing window. (If the file isn't yet stored on the device, DocsToGo retrieves it first.) You can also create a document to get started by tapping the plus-document icon in the lower corner of any file location view.

Tap in the text or cells for a Word or Excel doc, and you can start editing. The Undo and Redo buttons in the upper right help you recover from editing mistakes.

DocsToGo provides more limited options for editing PowerPoint presentations, and it's even a little opaque how to get started. Tap the up/down arrow icon at the bottom of a presentation you're editing, and then tap Outline View. This gives you access to the outline, but you're limited to formatting—such as including a bullet list—that's set in the template for each slide.

DocsToGo also works as a hub to collect your data from the various services

(see p. xviii)

MORE: The non-premium version ($9.99, **http://5str.us/ro7**) excludes Exchange, Dropbox, Box.net, SugarSync, and MobileMe iDisk, and PowerPoint creation and editing.

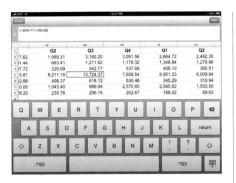

and servers across which files might be scattered. You can copy files via iTunes directly to the program, and retrieve them via the Local tab. Files created within DocsToGo are stored in the Local tab as well.

A Desktop tab gives you access to files over a local Wi-Fi network to sync with folders on local computers; this requires installation of a free program for Mac OS X and Windows, rather than using the standard WebDAV approach found in most other reading/editing apps. (The desktop program is a bit weak; I like to

browse folders, and the program was rather slow on a Mac.)

The Online view lets you connect to a variety of storage services, including Google Docs, Dropbox, SugarSync, and MobileMe iDisk. This option is excluded from the non-premium version, which costs $7 less. It's unlikely you'd want the cheaper version, because I can guarantee you'll want to have remote document access for editing and storage.

DocsToGo lets you bring documents in and out of other iOS apps: it should appear as an option in the Open In menu available now in many other programs for the formats it supports. And you can also—in reverse—have a document in DocsToGo open in another app that can read the file's format.

The app has built-in help (tap More, Settings, and then Help; it could use help to find Help), useful for a program with so many options.

Comics ▮▮

FREE • comiXology • http://5str.us/foy

The comic-reading engine powerful enough to leap (and pan) tall panels

The folks at comiXology power iOS comic reading with a special force, too powerful for one company to control: the Comics app. This program is available directly from comiXology (at no cost), and it's the same engine that underlies the Marvel Comics, DC Comics, and Scott Pilgrim apps.

By registering a comiXology account, you can read DC Comics and Scott Pilgrim books in the Comics app; Marvel has its own registration system. The reason to buy in the otherwise identical apps is to have access to newer content; the Comics app's store often has a couple-year lag on what it's able to offer.

Comics is organized into three simple tabs: My Comics, for free and paid comics you've downloaded or which are available to download on this device; Store, which lists free and priced comics; and Settings. The number of free

comics is quite high, with first issues special editons to promote a series or new release.

Both the My Comics and Store views offer a Browse button in the upper right that lets you look through your collection or available books by identifiers like series and publisher. Comics that you've bought but aren't downloaded to this device can be retrieved to Comics with a single tap on a red starburst. Tapping the Read button brings up the book.

comiXology's claim to fame is allowing pane-by-pane reading. Double-tap a pane, and then you tap or swipe to advance. For complicated layouts, the reader shows part of the layout at a time. Movement from pane to pane can involve balletic leaps, along with zooms in and out, as you tap to proceed. On an iPad, you can also read full screen and use pinch and expand gestures to make parts more legible or see more at once.

DC Comics

FREE • DC Comics • http://5str.us/9ng

Super heroes united on the digital page

The most iconic class of superheroes is found at DC Comics, home to Superman, Green Lantern, Wonder Woman, Flash, Batman, and a zillion others—I counted.

DC Comics' more adult line-ups are available—confusingly enough—only from the Comics app, not this one!

Marvel Comics

FREE • Marvel Entertainment • http://5str.us/zee

Metahumans, mutants, and Iron Man

The Marvel Universe's heroes tend towards magic, cosmic rays, and mutation, and we love them all: X-Men, Spiderman, Fantastic Four, the Hulk, and a host of others.

Scott Pilgrim

FREE • Bryan Lee O'Malley • http://5str.us/8pq

Battle seven evil ex-passwords to obtain the books

Scott Pilgrim Saves the World became one of the biggest serial hits of the graphic novel world. Following the simultaneous release of the movie and the sixth and final book in the series, this app appeared.

Scott Pilgrim lets you purchase the six books as in-app items ($6.99 for the first five and $11.99 for the final volume). Once purchased, you can use a comiXology account to read the stories in either this app or the Comics app.

NOTE: Ramona said seven evil-*exs*, not seven evil ex-boyfriends.

ComicZeal ▮▪

$7.99 • Bitolithic • http://5str.us/qbn

A virtual wallrack for comics

You might miss the feel of paper under your fingers as you flip through comics, but there's also something pleasant about having everything neatly at your disposal, as with ebooks. ComicZeal is a comics reader, handling several popular formats for packaging digital files into collections, including cbr, cbz, rar, zip, and PDF. (ComicZeal also acts as a PDF reader for any document, not just comics.)

A previous version of ComicZeal in iOS 3 required Wi-Fi syncing and other folderol to move items around. Now, you simply use iTunes File Sharing to copy files over USB (see p. xv). The Open In option in iOS 4 is also a conduit. You can use Dropbox, or any file-sharing program that opens remote files, to select a supported file format and then open it with ComicZeal. Safari also works: punch in a URL there or follow a link and ComicZeal should appear as an option to open the file.

Comics can be organized into collections or series, and the app is smart enough to read consistent file name patterns and drop new entrants into the right collection if they're labeled correctly. Collections have a nifty rack icon, too.

MORE: An iPhone/iPod touch compatible version is also available for $5.99 (**http://5str.us/8pv**).

To read a comic, you tap it, and it fills the screen. You can tap smack-dab in the center to toggle top and bottom navigation. On the bottom, there's an orientation lock for portrait or landscape mode. This avoids your comics lurching 90 degrees while you're reading. Buttons let you page back and forth in the book, and a slider moves rapidly.

Tap on the left and right sides to move back and forth without buttons. Pinch, expand, and pan gestures reveal page details. An "experimental" panning mode in settings tries to guess panel borders to zoom from one to the next.

Tap the settings icon at top (a wrench) to turn on assisted panning, and you're presented with possibly too many other options to adjust. But don't say that ComicZeal isn't trying to let you customize the reading experience to your precise delight. Set a background behind panels, and declutter the top and bottom navigation if you choose.

As to for how to find comics in these formats, look for free and paid sources of new comics all via the Web as well as an increasingly large horde of public domain titles. ComicZeal comes with a few, and offers links to download more.

2

Social Networking

No matter where you go, your friends can come with you. Social-networking apps let you have access to what your friends are up to—and where they are—when you're out and about, as well as giving you the medium to post your thoughts back to them.

Twitter ▪▫

FREE* • Twitter • http://5str.us/fbs

The operators of Twitter offer a strong entrant with a different feel

Should we be surprised that Twitter (the company) would release a great Twitter app? Not really. But what's surprising about this free entrant into the very crowded Twitter program market is how different it is from all the others. Even more fascinating is how different the iPhone/iPod touch version is from the iPad version—even though it's a universal app. (I prefer the iPad version.)

Both versions let you set up one or multiple Twitter accounts to follow the newest messages among those you follow, mentions of your Twitter name, and direct messages, among other features.

On the iPhone/iPod touch, Twitter works rather like many other apps, with separate views for accounts broken up by tweets, mentions, and direct messages. There's a lot of tapping involved in getting to a conversation thread, but it's workable.

The iPad version, however, truly shines in how it manages multiple frames of information. At first, it looks like just a side-by-side view: categories (like

Timeline and Search) at left, and tweets at right. But tap a tweet and the right pane slides over and a new pane overlays it showing the conversation (if any). That new pane that lets you navigate among profile information. Tap a URL in the timeline or in the profile pane, and a Web view slides in from the right.

When you want to dispose of the Web view, you give it a push or slide it back to the right. You can bring it back by swiping or dragging back to the left. The same is true of other panes, which snap to the right width as needed.

It's worth considering other Twitter apps on the iPhone, but Twitter for iPad has the lead on that hardware.

ACCOUNT: *Works with one or more Twitter accounts, but can also be used without an account to read public tweets and the public timeline.

Twitterific for Twitter

FREE* • The Iconfactory • http://5str.us/s73

Simple display of items from multiple Twitter accounts, suited for all devices

Twitterific was an early and fabulous Mac OS X Twitter client, and it's gone through three great overhauls iterations under iOS to reach its current form.

Every good Twitter app has a different focus. Twitterific's interest is in giving you a simplified and straightforward view of your tweets and those that are directed at you.

A main view—All Tweets—shows your timeline, highlighting direct messages and replies in separate colors to stand out. Green shows your own tweets; orange, a mention (in which your ID is shown); and gray, all other messages.

Tap names to get more details about a fellow tweeter, and follow threads. Threading lets you keep track of conversations.

The iPad version uses pop-over dialogs to show additional information when you tap, but works best in landscape mode, where the left side of the screen gives you more information than the iPhone version can display.

Along with writing tweets, you can take a picture or record a video on an iPhone, or choose an item from the Photo Library. Twitterific supports several image and video hosting services.

Contrariwise to Twitter's app, I prefer Twitterific on the iPhone/iPod touch; the iPad rendition is too spread out for me.

ACCOUNT: *Requires free Twitter account.

Birdhouse

$1.99* • Sandwich Dynamics • http://5str.us/cza

Compose and refine perfect tweets for later twittering

Birdhouse adds deliberation to Twitter by letting you compose and tweak tweets without having to post them immediately. While some Twitter clients now let you stores drafts, too, Birdhouse is 100-percent designed around the bon mot or clever phrase. That's why you'll see the Birdhouse client tag attached to tweets by many people who are—or sound—smart or funny. (Client tags are shown in small type on Twitter.com and in some other Twitter software.)

Birdhouse has a simple sheet where you write a tweet, with a character count in the lower right. You can add multiple accounts to Birdhouse, and choose from which account a tweet posts. You can also compose messages offline when no Internet access is available.

Tap the compose icon in the upper right, and write away. You can rank your own tweet from zero to five stars at the bottom, which shows up in the summary list, to remind yourself how marvelous one tweet is compared to another. A star tab in the list view lets you sort by star ranking.

Publishing and removing a tweet both involve deliberation, too. To post a tweet to your Twitter timeline, you can Publish, but then you have to tap Publish a second time to avoid posting prematurely if the first tap was a mistake.

Likewise, when you want to remove a tweet, you tap Unpublish, and then tap that again. Unpublishing a tweet deletes it from Twitter and places it back in draft status in Birdhouse.

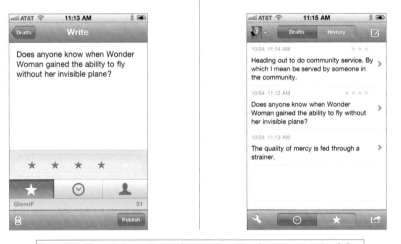

ACCOUNT: *Requires free Twitter account.

Facebook ▮▮

FREE* • Facebook • http://5str.us/mjl

Because you can't get enough Facebook at a fixed computer, have a mobile version

Sure, half a billion people use Facebook, but what if you can't gain access right this second? All is lost. No more! The official Facebook app is a well-constructed approach to reading and posting updates, viewing photos, and staying in touch—without throwing in the kitchen sink. It has restraint and utility.

The advantage and disadvantage of this mobile app is a lack of extra stuff that populates the Web site. You don't see ads (at least as of this writing), and there aren't constant reminders about friends you haven't connected with and suggestions of things, people, and places to interact with.

It's also missing access to Facebook applications. These Web-based apps aren't designed yet to run in the mobile world, and some require Flash. But a limited universe may be a good thing.

A main screen offers nine links for common activities, with News Feed at the upper left. You can access photos, your profile, a list of friends, and more. A second page has just a single link, and you can add links (tap the + sign) from your friends or any Facebook pages you've liked.

You can leave comments, "Like" things, and check in using Places at locations near you. Places finds the nearest spots if you let it use your current position. You can also approve friend requests, make new ones, and chat.

ACCOUNT: *Requires Facebook account, which is free.

Tumblr

FREE* • Tumblr • http://5str.us/jl8

View your timeline and add posts and media with ease

Tumblr users revel in posting all kinds of things—audio, video, links, text, and more—and this app obliges. Keeping it simple, the program sports two tabs: Post and Dashboard. Tap Post and you can quickly add media, text, and other supported types. You can record new audio and video or snap a photo, or upload existing material.

The Dashboard tab shows the latest information in your Tumblr timeline: a collection of all the items posted by yourself and anyone you follow. The timeline lets you edit your own posts by tapping, or "like" or reblog someone else's entry.

You can post to and view entries from multiple accounts with this app.

WordPress

FREE* • Automattic • http://5str.us/d3v

Post entries to a WordPress blog with text, photos, tags—and no fuss

The WordPress app does an able job of providing access to the most common features you might need while making a blog post and not sitting in front of a computer.

Instead of loading the app with the million features accessible from a WordPress posting page or dashboard, the app offers you a way to post, to edit static pages, and to view and moderate comments.

The WordPress app takes advantage of the mobile hardware, letting you geotag a post (i.e., use coordinates for where you are), and pull in stored photos or snap a picture. You can upload video from an iPhone or latest iPod touch.

The app also supports multiple Word-Press accounts in case you have or contribute to more than one blog.

3

AUDIO & MUSIC

A mobile device can provide music on demand, whether it's stored in memory or streaming over a Wi-Fi or cellular network. You can also make beautiful music of your own. The apps in this chapter stream, share, connect, and sing.

Pandora ▢▪

FREE • Pandora Media • http://5str.us/tno

Endless radio stations of your composition with optional ads

Open Pandora and you don't release all the evils of the world—nor a little hope. (You don't turn blue and tall, either.) Rather, you unchain an endless number of custom streaming radio stations that aim to match your likes.

You start by creating an account, which gives the firm some of your demographic information. Pandora is funded by advertising: you're trading personal data for free music.

In the Pandora app, start creating custom stations. Tap the New Station icon at the bottom. In the Artist tab, enter a song title, artist name, or composer. The Genre tab lets you choose from several broad categories.

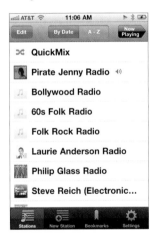

Pandora uses your selected song, artist, or composer as a jumping off point. For instance, I am a fan of the song "Die Seeräuber Jenny" ("Pirate Jenny") from *The Threepenny Opera*. When I tap

in that song title, Pandora offers me several different versions. I select Nina Simone's, and the "Pirate Jenny Radio" station that I just crevated starts off by playing that artist singing a song from *Porgy & Bess*.

Tap the detail button while a song is playing (the bullet list icon in the upper right), and the Song tab exposes some of the logic that the Pandora system used in picking that particular number. Pandora uses a system called the Music Genome Project that attempts to match common elements across songs.

You can try to fine-tune Pandora's results by tapping the thumbs up or thumbs down button. This works, but only to a certain extent. You can also skip a song, but not go back.

Because Pandora is a streaming service, you can run through cellular data if you listen to it constantly away from

---

MORE: Pandora lets you opt out of ads by paying $36 per year via the company Web site.

a Wi-Fi network. The app is designed to minimize 3G data use, and work at a higher quality over Wi-Fi networks. Pandora can play as a background app in iOS 4.

ooTunes Radio
$4.99 • OOgli • http://5str.us/bep

Every streaming station in the world and then some at your fingertips

ooTunes is a conduit to the vast number of streaming radio stations available worldwide. The app, which supports iOS 4 background audio, provides a number of discovery tools to browse and find stations that match your interest.

The list includes both broadcast radio stations that have streaming feeds and Internet-only radio stations. The bit rate is shown alongside stations; that's the amount of data that's sent, with a lower number working better over slower

connections and consuming less bandwidth. Stations you like can be marked as favorites to find more easily the next time you launch the program.

The program also lets you plug in account information for the streaming Internet versions of Sirius Radio and XM Radio, and live365 VIP (an ad-free paid version of that service).

ooTunes has an alarm clock option to let you wake up to a station of your choosing. You can play Radio "RooLette" to have random songs plucked out and played for you.

AOL Radio
FREE • AOL • http://5str.us/jqr

Free access to CBS Radio's broadcast and streaming stations

AOL Radio lets you tune in to CBS Radio stations. CBS Radio operates over 200 terrestrial broadcast stations around the United States, and also offers 25 streaming format stations. The app can use location to find those nearest you.

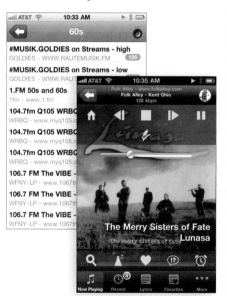

QUp

$0.99 • Dan Pourhadi • http://5str.us/vry

Manage an active list of music on the fly straight-through or shuffled

QUp is an app that, before you use it, you don't know you need it. The program provides extremely fine and well-considered control over creating and managing a persistent playlist of music. It fills in missing pieces in the iPod app.

The software is like one super playlist. You select music to add from a music view that shows your whole audio library (podcasts excluded), listing Playlists, Albums, Artists, and Songs. The More view adds Compilations, Composers, and Genres.

From any display, you drill down to songs or albums, and can tap a + next to Add All Songs (including at the top level to add all your music) or tap a + next to any individual song.

Tap Done, and the list is ready to go. The play view shows album cover art (where available) filling the screen. If you tap that view, the bottom half previews the next track with an album cover, the song title, its album name, and the artist.

You can advance back and forth through upcoming songs and tap to jump to the track you've selected. And you can turn shuffle play on and off as well from this view.

Tap the list icon at upper right, and you can review and manipulate the songs you've chosen. Tap a song to move it to the top of the queue without interrupting music that's playing. Tap the Shuffle button and you can resort the whole list and see the results.

The list view also lets you see a compendium of artists and albums, and search among the items in the playlist.

The software's only substantial missing feature is the ability to save custom QUp playlists you can bring back to play again later.

CONSIDERATION: QUp can't play music protected by DRM, which means any audio you purchased from the iTunes Store before Apple stopped selling protected albums and songs.

Airfoil Speakers Touch ▪▪▫

FREE* • Rogue Amoeba Software • http://5str.us/2r7

Pass audio from computers running Airfoil to your iOS device

Think of Airfoil Speakers Touch as turning an iOS device into a portable speaker. The app works with Rogue Amoeba's Airfoil commercial software for Mac OS X and Windows. Airfoil captures and redirects audio that's playing on a computer to a variety of devices: other computers, AirPort Express, Apple TV, and mobile hardware running this iOS app.

For Airfoil Speakers Touch to work, your iOS device must be on the same Wi-Fi network as the computer from which you want to stream audio.

Setup is simple. Install Airfoil on a computer on the network, launch the Airfoil Speakers Touch app, and select the device as a destination from the computer software. Because the app supports background audio, it continues to play music even if you switch to another program. If you're on a shared network,

you can still stream without fear of others listening in—you may not want them to know that you've got Depeche Mode on infinite shuffle—by setting a password in Settings within the app.

Airfoil Speakers Touch works as a perfect complement to remote control apps. With Apple's free Remote app (see p. 175), you can control iTunes on the same computer that's streaming audio from Airfoil to your iOS device. You can also use the app to create remote headphones. While watching a video across the room shunt the audio to your iOS device and plug in earphones.

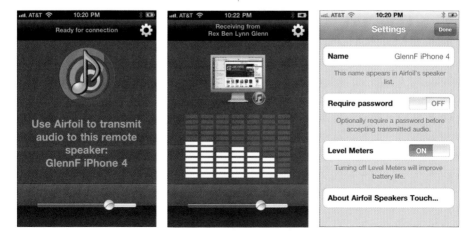

REQUIREMENT: *Paid desktop software must be installed on the same network. A demo version of the desktop software is available. It works for a short time for each session.

Ocarina ▮▮▪

$0.99 • Smule • http://5str.us/5dm

Unearthly music by blowing on the microphone

One of the earliest iPhone apps to get attention after Apple opened up its operating system to outside developers was Ocarina from Ge Wang, a Stanford University professor. You blow into the microphone as if it were a wind instrument—the ancient ocarina, to be exact.

As you blow, you cover or uncover combinations of four virtual openings on the touch screen. Despite the simplicity of the instrument you can play complex songs. (It works better without a case, which can make it hard to handle the phone as an instrument.)

You can tune Ocarina via the app's settings to other keys and to Greek modes like Ionian. (A little joke about the game *The Legend of Zelda* is thrown in with Zeldarian being one mode you can select.)

You can opt not to use a mic or headset by setting Touch Mode to On. This produces all tones at the same volume instead of responding to the amount of breath. (That's the only choice for the iPod touch.)

All the software from Smule (or SonicMule) has a social component as well. In Ocarina's case, you can tap a globe icon and hear people playing all over the world, some quite expertly. Tap the heart icon, and you've contributed toward a particular player moving into Top Melodies as well as adding them to your My Loved list.

You might wonder how you teach yourself to play songs on the Ocarina. The answer can be found on SonicMule's Web site, where sheet music uniquely transcribed for Ocarina can be found. The form takes just a moment to learn.

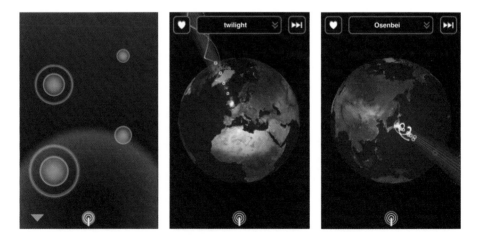

Glee

$0.99 • Smule • http://5str.us/1ec

If you sing in the shower, you don't have to love *Glee* to love this app

Conceive of the original Guitar Hero mashed up with karaoke, and you've figured out the Glee app from Smule. While you sing along with the instrumentals of songs culled from the show, starbursts explode as you sing. A visual display of the relative pitch of the note gives you feedback as you fix your pitch.

Miss the notes, and you can opt to have your singing auto-tuned electronically altered to fit the right note, no matter what you sing.

Rack up starbursts (which count as points) and compete on a daily basis with other Gleekers—fans of the show—worldwide. Or you can just sing for yourself.

Your performance can be recorded, and you can listen to yourself. And you can send a copy of the song to others via email or upload to Facebook, tweet it, or post it on MySpace.

The app includes a few songs at no cost, and you can buy additional tunes for 99¢ each. I recommend "Bohemian Rhapsody"and "Dream On."

Your song can also be "broadcast," or uploaded to a central Glee repository, which requires a free account.

Smule's apps are all about sharing, and *Glee* is a worldwide phenomenon. Tap a Listen button on the home screen, and choose people performing with the app all over the world, join in on songs as another singer, and invite complete strangers (as well as friends) to be co-vocalists on a track.

The app brings all of the best aspects of karaoke singing (including showing you the lyrics) with tonal correction (and optional reverb). Even better: with the benefit of anonymity, sing out unselfconsciously. Go ahead: belt a tune! We won't judge you.

TIP: Glee is best enjoyed with headphones and an in-line mic.
WARNING: Listening to yourself sing can be a humbling experience, but this app can teach you to sing better.

Magic Piano ■■ ∎

$0.99 • Smule • http://5str.us/z7s

A piano without keys

Magic Piano is more of an approxima-tion of the sense of a piano than a literal intrepretation. The app allows enjoyable exploration of notes and melodies, but I wouldn't recommend you try to play a tune. (They all laughed when I sat down to play!)

The program features four keyboards, all of them a bit strange, but interesting. You tap the circular key icon at the upper right to cycle through them.

The keyboards are a spiral, a straight line (with undulations), a circle, and invisible. In each mode, you can tap mul-tiple keys at the same time to produce chords. (An iPad can record up to about 10 separate finger taps at once, and Magic Piano works with that.)

The spiral and circle modes are just for playing around, while you can experi-ment with real music in the straight keyboard. With the circle or straight layout, pinch and expand to change the number of keys (and their width) shown on screen. Swipe left and right to move up and down the keyboard.

The menu offers other interesting options, like Songbook. The app down-loads a score for a song you select from a modest list, like *Pictures at an Exhibition*. Notes start descending as spots of light from top to bottom. Tap the spot in the order of descent, and you're playing the song.

When you play, your music is beamed out to the rest of the world (using a name you enter in Settings). You can lis-ten in through the World option, or join in by tapping Duet. That mode matches you up with someone likewise seeking a partner. Your respective positions are shown on a globe while you play.

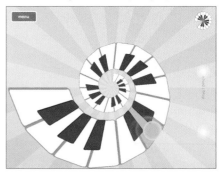

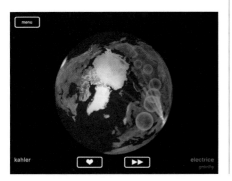

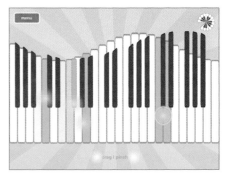

NOTE: The invisible keyboard option works just the same as the Songbook mode only without notes dripping down.

Soundrop ▮▮

FREE • Develoe • http://5str.us/ju3

Magical musical effects by drawing lines that act as chords for bouncing balls

Fascinating patterns emerge from simple actions. That's the key to understanding (and loving) minimalist music from artists like Steven Reich, and the key to falling in love with Soundrop.

Soundrop has no goal. Rather, a ball drops, and you draw lines. The lines are chords; the length affects the tone produced when the line is hit. Longer lines produce deeper notes.

The balls bounce off the lines with some semblance of physics (with very low gravity) to produce melodies controlled by changing the angle and length of lines. You can produce fast-moving cacophonies, or slow, ponderous dirges.

The free version lets you explore simple notes. An in-app upgrade adds four elements: multiple instruments, which you assign to different colors used to draw lines; physics modifiers to change gravity, friction, and bounciness; the ability

to drop multiple balls at once; and the option to save a "game," so you can restore your melody.

While Soundrop doesn't have a goal and there is no scoring, you strive with the app to make interesting music instead of noise. Which may be the purpose of life itself.

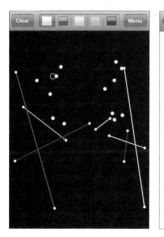

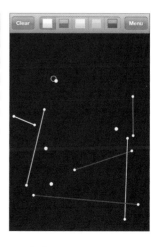

UPGRADE: The free version can be upgraded via an in-app purchase ($1.99) for enhanced features.

4

Photography

You are a camera.

Carrying an iPhone or newest iPod touch means there's never a time you aren't ready to take a picture. But is the picture ready for you? In this chapter, learn how to make an ordinary photo extraordinary, get playful, and view the results.

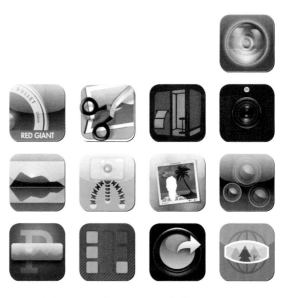

EFFECTS / FLICKR / PANORAMAS / SHOT CONTROL / ADAPTERS / FUN / CORRECTION

Hipstamatic

$1.99 • Synthetic Infatuation • http://5str.us/vwx

Use classic camera treatments and effects to punch up standard iPhone pictures

Photographers of any vintage will tell you that the film is part of what makes the picture. So are the lens and the camera body. You may frame the shot, set the exposure, and choose the right time, but photos have always been a result of unpredictable outcomes from all the factors that go into them.

Hipstamatic tries to put some of those combinations under glass by aptly mimicking the lens effects of particular camera models, the color and development peculiarities of particular films, and the filter and cast of flashes.

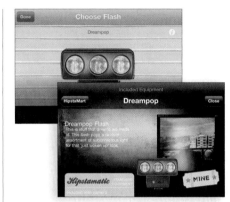

All pictures are taken with the Hipstamatic 150 camera body (a tip of the hat to a 30-year-old model), which offers three lenses, three films, and two flash choices. More sets of camera, flashes, and films can be purchased in-app for 99¢ each.

When setting up a shot, the app lets you choose among the camera options you own. Tap the turn-around arrow at lower right to make selections. The icons along the bottom correspond to film, flash, and lenses. Tap any of them,

and you can swipe back and forth among what's available. (It's also a sales pitch for items you don't own, with access to the in-app store from the same view.) Tap any specialty item, like a flash, and the screen fills with detailed information about what kind of results to expect. Tap the turn-around arrow again to return to the main camera view and take photos.

You frame pictures in a sort of cleverly awkward way: the viewfinder only shows you part of the image area, which means you're working more roughly, but can produce happy accidents. You can turn this off and see the entire framed area,

REQUIREMENTS: An iOS device with a camera.

but you may like it better with the view-finder cropping; I thought it added randomness. (Launch the Settings app and swipe to the Hipstamatic icon.)

From the camera side, swipe the flash bottom to "power it up," and tap the big yellow button to take a picture. A Developing label appears for a moment, and then you need to wait for the green Print Ready light to wink on at the lower left. (The verisimilitude may wear thin after a few of those.)

Tap the photo square to view pictures, which are always framed as squares. From the photo view, you can create collections of images (called stacks), which can be emailed, or shared on Facebook, Flickr, or a Tumblr site. You can also order prints in sets of 9 or 27, with any quantity for each image.

NOTE: Maynard G. Krebs not included (**http://5str.us/uho**).

Panoramatic 360 ▆▆ ▪

$1.99 • Floaty • http://5str.us/pa6

Complex settings reward with well-rendered panoramas and a community

Panoramatic 360 is a bit more complicated to use than two of the panorama apps on the following pages, but it produces more precise results, both to help you take the correct overlapping images and to create a final picture. For those who want a high level of control, this app is highly recommended.

You start by choosing either a portrait or landscape orientation to take photos, or pick a photo from your device's library instead.

When working with live images, choose the starting place for the panorama and take the first shot. The app helps align subsequent photos, which are added to the right. A small overlap is shown from the previous photo at the left to assist in making a good match. You can turn on an audio hinter or a set of gridlines to help out.

To keep orientation and alignment for any shot (but especially critical for 360-degree panorama), a circle with two dots aids you. A yellow dot shows how far out of alignment you are in the circle; make small adjustments in position and angle until the overlap of the image is perfect and the yellow dot is as close to on top of the blue dot as possible.

For either live pictures or those that are being built out of your existing photos, you can add pictures on either end of the panorama in a review mode. When you tap Finish, you have basic and advanced options for correcting the image. These options can be a little involved, and experimentation is useful.

PICTURED: Bottom, the George Washington Memorial Bridge (Aurora Bridge) in the Fremont neighborhood of Seattle.

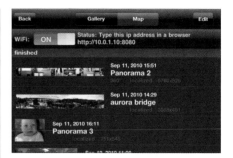

The built-in help instructions provide details about the settings (including adjusting exposure and correcting for lens distortion), but help can't be accessed while you're adjusting settings. Tap Save Project to save the state of your work, read the help, and then use the Gallery view's Drafts section to retrieve your project. Now you can test results by changing settings and tapping Render. Large projects can take a few minutes to produce.

The resulting images can be saved in the local photo library, emailed (at lower resolution), or retrieved over a local network using WebDAV sharing (see p. xvi for more on WebDAV]. You can also contribute panoramas to the app's worldwide directory, Panoramatic World. (Tap a link on the home page to view other people's work by name or on a map, and rate it, too.)

The Gallery view lets you review your stored panoramas, see where they were taken on a world map, and manage Wi-Fi sharing.

PICTURED: At top, a brunch with my kids, my wife, and her parents.

Pano

$2.99 • Debacle Software • http://5str.us/s14

Simple but effective way to create panoramas

Pano has one function: start making a panorama, advance to the right to match an overlap shown, and tap again. When you're done, tap a checkmark and wait from about 20 seconds (for four images) to a couple minutes (for a full 360°). The results are quite lovely, and automatically saved into the photo roll.

I recommend Pano for users who want the least amount of fiddling and fuss, despite the extra dollar more than Panoramatic 360. The less expensive program rewards more time spent with it; Pano has a very shallow learning curve to achieve great results.

360 Panorama

$2.99 • Occipital • http://5str.us/o7y

A panorama forms as your hand moves

Wave your hands in the air like you really do care—care enough to pan your iPhone or 4th-generation iPod touch around slowly to capture a sphere that encompasses you.

360 Panorama doesn't require aligning edges to stitch images together, nor does it render in a fancy way. Rather, the app works hard at the time it's capturing images, which are taken continuously, to create a seamless panorama based on motion and image analysis. It's awfully good for the difficult task at hand.

REQUIREMENTS: Pano requires an iOS device with a camera.
PICTURED: Bottom, Aurora Bridge/Fremont Bridge, Seattle, assembled in Pano; top, my home in 360 Panorama.

Options are few: you can choose to create a kind of overhead torus that splays out the continuous image as if you were flattening a globe (stereographic), or have a long strip (equirectangular). Images are saved automatically to the Camera Roll.

You Gotta See This!

$1.99 • Boinx Software •
http://5str.us/1u7

Assemble photos into a loose panorama or a collection of tiles with no tapping

You Gotta See This is a quasi-panorama app: it produces panoramic-like images that aren't perfectly stitched together,

but are rather lovely in any case. Its big advantage is that no tapping is required nor any alignment of overlaps.

The results are more impressionistic than precise, but the pictures have quite a bit of charm. You have more options for how pictures are rendered than any of the other apps, too.

Tap the Camera icon on the main screen, and start slowly moving the camera around. When done, tap the Camera icon again, and a preview appears in the Light Table Collage style. That mode imperfectly but attratively overlaps photos in the rough physical layout in which they were taken. Six other styles are available, including tiled versions.

You can save the final image to the Camera Roll, share on Twitter or Facebook, or send as email.

REQUIREMENTS: You Gotta See This! requires an iPhone 4 or 4th-generation iPod touch.
PICTURED: You Gotta See This! panoramas: top, Aurora Bridge, Seattle; right middle, brunch with family.

IncrediBooth ■■

$0.99 • Synthetic • http://5str.us/j2i

A photobooth in your pocket with all the charm

Despite once being chemically scalded by an instant photo-strip booth near the Eiffel Tower—we came out unscathed, fortunately—I still have a soft spot in my heart for this antiquated instant photography.

For a handful of quarters, the old booths would snap four black-and-white photos of you and friends in quick succession as you crammed into a small space and mugged. A few moments later, a developed strip pop`ped out the side. (Those photostrips are a plot point in the movie *Amélie*.)

IncrediBooth does a marvelous job of re-creating the experience of a photobooth without your having to carry around an inconveniently large object. The app uses the front-facing camera of an iPhone 4 or newest iPod touch.

There are no options, really. Press the button, watch the light blink, and pose, pose, pose, pose. A moment later slide over to the output tray, and the strip plunks down. You can save the resulting image (which is created as a single image file) to the Camera Roll, email it, or upload it to Facebook.

REQUIREMENTS: An iPhone 4 or 4th-generation iPod touch.

Gorillacam ■■

FREE • Joby • http://5str.us/rw5

Enhances your ability to line up photos and shoot them rapid fire

Gorillacam brings several features to taking pictures that mimic options on a camera. Apple doesn't include these features for simplicity's sake, but having them available (and at no cost) makes an iPhone more of a camera.

The app provides an onscreen grid and a level bubble to straighten or at least frame photos. One option lets you tap anywhere to take a picture, instead of using just the tiny camera button. You can also set a timer, take time-lapse pictures, and adjust for camera shake.

One feature I particularly like and use regularly is the three-shot burst. Unlike the new HDR (high dynamic range) feature in the iPhone 4 camera system, which combines multiple shots at different exposures, the three-shot burst takes three pictures as quickly as the app can, storing them separately.

With iOS 4, Gorillacam was able to fix one small problem in previous releases: the app takes longer to save photos than Apple's built-in Camera app, and needed extra time to save. If you exited before saving, photos could be lost. With iOS 4, the app can ask iOS to finish up what it's doing.

You might note that several of these features seem to require a way to keep an iPhone or iPod touch still. That's because Joby also sells very nifty camera mounts with flexible legs, including one designed for iOS devices: the Gorillamobile series (**http://5str.us/t5e**).

REQUIREMENTS: Any iOS device with a camera.

CameraBag

$1.99 • Nevercenter • http://5str.us/262

Simulate classic camera lenses on and apply effects to your photos

Nostalgia is often tinted, and Camera-Bag provides the means to evoke it. The app can apply effects to a picture taken using the iPhone or latest iPod touch's camera; you can also select an image from any iOS device's photo library. You choose among filters, some of which also crop the photo.

Some filters are camera styles, like Helga, Lolo, and Plastic (referring to a plastic lens). Others apply effects, like Fisheye, Infrared, and Mono. CameraBag goes even further, with effects that ape a particular photographic feel, such as 1962, 1974, or Magazine. You can tap to change filters, or swipe to cycle through them.

CameraBag has you set the resolution of the output photo before you save it to the device's library or email the photo. The higher the resolution, the longer it takes to run the original through the filter. (What it shows onscreen is a preview.)

Why use CameraBag? When you want to transform the look of something into another era or appearance and want a consistent outcome. Other apps offer similar features, but focus on variability.

The iPad version (shown above) allows you to set border, filter, and cropping separately, and tap a Vary button to make random variations in a filter type.

MORE: CameraBag is also available for the iPad ($2.99, **http://5str.us/86q**). A desktop version of the software (Mac and Windows) offers somewhat more capabilities in the same vein.

Best Camera ■■

$2.99 • Chase Jarvis Worldwide • http://5str.us/f3c

See through to a photo's essential nature

Chase Jarvis, a photographer who inspires other photographers, released Best Camera to allow the small changes to pictures that often make photos pop. Best Camera has no fancy features. It can make images starker by removing colors or more vivid by enhancing saturation.

After taking a picture in the app or loading one from the Photo Library, swipe along the bottom to look through filters. Filters are additive: keep applying them to layer effects. Tap the filter icon in the upper right and a display of all the applied effects appears at the bottom; tap an X to remove a given change.

The program, which takes its name from the motto, "the best camera is the one that's with you," also hooks into several photo-sharing and social-networking services. With a single tap, you can upload to Flickr, post to Facebook, tweet at Twitter, save to your Camera Roll, and email the image out—and send a copy to Jarvis's **thebestcamera.com** site. Photos on that site are accessible via the app, too, in a nifty photo-reveal interface.

Best Camera may help you become a better photographer by giving you a few controls in the field to make the iPhone a better, if not best, camera.

TIP: Chase Jarvis has a book published by Peachpit Press also called **The Best Camera Is the One That's with You**. It's full of photos taken and adjusted with the app that should inspire you, too (**http://5str.us/l4k**).

Plastic Bullet ▪▪

$1.99 • Red Giant Software • http://5str.us/glz

Charming variants of a plastic camera lens at a tap

Film cameras with plastic lenses produce distorted pictures with inaccurate color, but which have a weirdly fascinating aesthetic. Parts of what you capture that seem banal in the real world become something else through a plastic lens.

Plastic Bullet simulates a plastic-lens camera, an effect or feature in several other apps in the book. Plastic Bullet's simplicity may recommend it, as well as its "variant" button.

Choose a picture from your photo library, or take a photo, and the app creates four variants. Tap a reload button, and four more are created. You can continue on this merry way indefinitely, producing an original effect each time.

Choose the variant you like, tap a heart button, and save it to the photo roll. You can also choose to upload to Facebook and Flickr.

Photogene

$1.99 • Omer Shoor • http://5str.us/7sd

Sophisticated photo correction in a small package

Photogene is a tool for those with a mild to serious interest in image correction. The app has features recognizable to anyone who has ever needed to use a desktop program like Adobe Photoshop or Elements for fixing color shift, adjusting white balance, and redistributing light and dark through levels.

Start by loading a picture from your Photo Library or taking a picture if your device has a built-in camera.

Photogene divides its manipulations into several categories, some of which are corrections, while others are special effects or overlays.

Crop and rotate commands let you take a photo and trim it, rotate it, straighten it, or flip it. A filter option lets you choose sharpening, a way of improving the crispness of a picture when used in moderation, or from a number of special effects, like turning the image into a sepia-toned photo.

The color adjust view offers full-on levels adjustment in which you can change the overall distribution of light and dark

across a photo. It also allows simpler contrast/brightness adjustment, which I haven't recommended using since 1991, and some color tweaking.

The symbols and frames views seem a bit out of place with this app's other features: you can add cartoon balloons or stars, or choose a frame around an image. I'd avoid these.

When you're done adjusting, tap the checkmark. You can adjust the dimensions of the resulting photo choosing from a list (which shows the widest or tallest side) or entering your own value.

The app caters to professionals in the Share menu, allowing the inclusion of IPTC tagging and an option to include or exclude geotagging coordinates.

You can share the photos in several ways: via Twitter, Facebook, or Flickr, or to an FTP account on a server, as well as copying it or emailing the picture.

MORE: Photogene is also available for the iPad ($3.99, **http://5str.us/i74**).

Flickpad Pro ▪▪▪

$4.99 • Shacked Software • http://5str.us/zrc

Natural exploration of Flickr photos from you and your friends

I have thousands of photos on Flickr, but I've never been a fan of its Web site for looking through my own pictures (in sets or individually) or those of my Flickr contacts. (My contacts are a combination of friends, family, colleagues, and minor celebrities.) FlickPad Pro is a terrific way to explore, allowing me to revisit my own work and browse through others'.

When launched, the app first shows a simulation of a stack of photos, all a bit askew, overlapping one another. This pile is drawn from the most recent photos in both your photostream and those photostreams of your contacts. You can drag photos around to see them better. Holding down on a picture brings it to the top of the stack.

If you flick a photo offscreen, another replaces it. Use two fingers to flick, and all the photos from that contact disappear. (A number of tap and swipe

shortcuts are available, neatly laid out when you tap the i button at the top.)

You can also hold down on a picture to take actions: email the photo, mark all that contact's photos as seen (which removes them from the main page), or hide that contact to prevent his or her photos from appearing without "reactivating" them via the Settings menu.

Double-tap a photo, and the contact's sets are loaded. Double-tap a set, and the photos are revealed. Tap any photo,

MORE: A more limited free version, Flickpad Lite, is also available (**http://5str.us/pfy**).

and the image fills the screen, showing the caption and date at lower left.
At upper right, a star or favorite button
lets you mark an image as one you like
and see others who did the same. A
comments button shows comments and
allows you to leave new comments, too.
Tap Slideshow and the current set is displayed in sequence.

 ### Flickr Studio

$4.99* • Keeple •
http://5str.us/9dp

**A perfect interface for interacting with
Flickr on an iPad**

Flickr Studio takes a different and
equally valid approach to filtering Flickr
photos for viewing on an iPad. Where
Flickpad Pro homes in on sets and contacts, Flickr Studio's focus is more on
time and place.

Flickr incorporates quite a bit of information about each photo that's uploaded
to the service, including geographic
coordinates if the picture was taken
with a camera or mobile phone that
embeds that information. You can also

add location details from the Flickr Web
site for photos that lack latitude and
longitude.

Flickr Studio navigates among all this
embedded and added information. The
app's home page shows a grid of your
photos (after you log in with an account),
with callouts showing the dates for each
batch. Swipe over photos and hold to see
a larger thumbnail; tap to view the picture at full size.

Flickr Studio lets you explore quite
readily, too, with tabs for your contacts'
photos, for Flickr's interesting photos of
the day, and for pictures available from
institutions that offer images for viewing
and describing.

A map mode lets you both explore
photos around you or anywhere in the
world. If you're viewing pictures and
switch into the map mode—available in
several places in the app—tiny thumbnails cluster around where those photos
were taken. Tap to view.

Paid Flickr Pro users can view photos at
the full stored resolution. Like Flickpad
Pro, Flickr Studio doesn't upload pictures; they're all about viewing.

ACCOUNT: *Requires a free or paid Flickr account.

iPad Camera Connection Kit

$29.00 • Apple • http://5str.us/j37

Great tool for bringing pictures directly from a camera into an iPad

The iPad doesn't have a camera—or at least, the models available when I write this lack any—but you can still use an iPad to view images in the Photos app and manipulate them with software covered earlier in this chapter.

One way to do this is to sync albums, places, faces, and other collections between iPhoto on a Mac and your iPad. But you can also bring images directly into the iPad.

Apple offers the Camera Connection Kit to import pictures from a digital camera or Secure Digital (SD) memory card. The kit has two pieces, both of which plug into the standard Dock connector at the bottom of the iPad. One of the adapters has a USB jack at the other end; the other adapter is an SD card reader with a slot for that format of card.

When you plug in an adapter and either attach a supported digital camera or plug in an SD card, the Photos app launches, and you can choose to import some or all of the photos with an optional delete of the original. The full-resolution images are now resident in the iPad. You can forward them, upload them, and work with them more or less like any other image.

Because an iPhone or iPod touch also can act like a photo repository when either is plugged in via USB, you can perform the strange and unnatural act of connecting one of these smaller iOS devices to an iPad using the kit and import photos.

If you're set up to sync with iPhoto on a Mac, the pictures you uploaded should be copied over the next time you sync.

With a 3G iPad and an active data plan, importing photos via the adapters can let you post pictures when you're away from a computer and Wi-Fi network access. I've posted pictures when on trips just for fun.

You might think, "Hey, Apple has just given me a USB port! I should plug all kinds of things in!" Surprisingly, many USB devices can work with an iPad without official support. I've tested keyboards, external mic headsets, and speakers, and they all function. I've used a USB headset to make Skype calls. It's unwieldy, but works.

Apple doesn't offer a list of support digital cameras, but it appears that nearly all models are supported from major manufacturers.

NOTE: No, neither adapter is recognized by an iPhone or iPod touch, at least not at this writing. Yes, I've tried with both the phone and the music player.

5

Video Games

Pew! Pew! Pew! I got 'em.

Video games come in all shapes and sizes.
Guys that run and jump. Zombies that attack.
Balls that must be flicked. Cars that round tracks.
The common aspect is action. You cause an action
and a result occurs. There's often (but not always)
little chance to reflect in the middle of a video game,
as a contrast to games of strategy or word games.

Act now!

Trism ■■■

$2.99 • Demiforce • http://5str.us/ppp

Addictive, absorptive game involving lining up the right triangles across three axes

Trism was one of the first iPhone break-out games that everyone was suddenly downloading and playing. Its essence is simple. You're presented with a screen of equilateral triangles of different colors. You move triangles as a ribbon that wraps around the edges either diagonally left or right, or horizontally.

Line up three or more triangles across adjacent faces, and they're removed. As in Bejeweled (p. 55), a game to which Trism owns more than a glance, assembling a set of more than three triangles provides bigger rewards, and certain patterns are allotted badges, displayed on a trophies page. Matches cascade for more points as pieces removed for one match slide other sets of three or more triangles into new matches.

There are three modes of game play. Untimed gameplay is called Infinism and a timed mode is Terminism. Challenges are inserted, such as a bomb that has to be cleared in a set number of moves.

The third mode is more intriguing. Syllogism is a set of levels in which you slide pieces together in the least number of moves. Gameplay uses device tilting to move all the free pieces in a given direction at once. Scoring is based on least moves to achieve the objective.

You can optionally create an account to share scores with a global leaderboard, or keep your obsession to yourself.

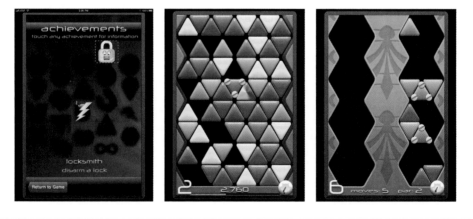

Bejeweled 2 + Blitz

$2.99 • PopCap • http://5str.us/37g

The original jewel-dropping mind virus gets even better

If any game is a mind virus, it's Bejeweled. The original incarnation dates back to the Palm Pilot, where I whiled away many obsessed hours lining up and swapping jewels to drop rows. Bejeweled 2 + Blitz adds two new game modes and a multiplayer option hooked up via Facebook.

The point of Bejeweled is simple. Jewels drop from the top into a grid. Swap adjacent jewels (left/right or top/bottom) to get three, four, or five in a row vertically or horizontally. And suddenly it's three hours later.

The original game rewarded you with points for lining up three or more jewels, and that mode of play is still available as Classic. Cascades of three jewels—where removing one set of three plus triggers removing subsequent sets of matched gems—earn even greater points.

In Action and Endless modes, line up four jewels and you prime a trigger that blows up a number of surrounding jewels on the next 3-or-more connection. Line up five jewels and a scintillating gem forms that can, when swapped with an adjacent jewel, zap all same-colored ones on the screen.

Blitz mode gives you one minute to score as high as you can. Blitz uses Facebook for sharing and connection, and lets you check scores against friends, track your score performance over the last five weeks, and brag by posting badges.

In Blitz, you can also buy performance-enhancing extras, like a "mystery gem," five extra seconds, and so forth.

The Facebook version of this app is tied in. If you visit Facebook, you can spin a wheel and earn more coins that you can spend in the Blitz mode of the app.

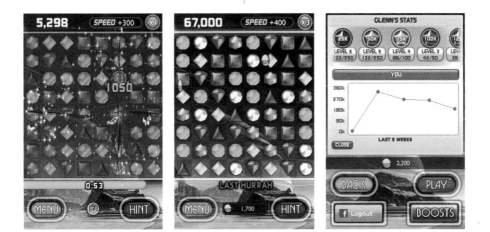

TIP: Get three in a row in crossing rows and one gem is turned into a blasting jewel. When that's matched with two or more of the same type, the gem blows up and destroys a full row and column.

Peggle

$2.99 • PopCap Games • http://5str.us/xr1

Like pachinko, pinball, and Bejeweled all in one, with spirit (level) guides

The makers of Bejeweled, PopCap Games, know a lot about how to get you addicted. With Peggle, the game trades out speed for complexity, which leads to compulsion. Your goal is to clear orange pegs on a game board. The game space has up-down orientation, and balls obey gravity. The board is more like pachinko than pinball, but has aspects of both.

The balls are shot from the top using a funnel you can aim by tapping. A fine-tune dial at right lets you adjust the pitch in tiny increments. A little set of aiming guidelines is painted as you move the funnel around to predict where the ball will go. One bonus provides exact and extended aiming prediction.

Green and purple pegs add special tools and bonus points. In a crab level, one bonus gives you crab claw paddles at either side of the bottom to bounce balls back into play.

Starting with a unicon, 10 "Peggle masters" move you through 55 levels, offering advice between turns about clearing levels, scoring bonus points, and the zen of the game.

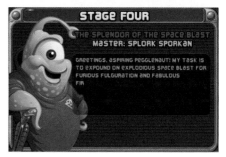

You receive extra points for all manner of activities, from a long shot (a bounce across the board that knocks out an orange peg), to stylish plays, to dropping a ball into a moving pan at the bottom. That pan also grants an extra ball, and the game sometimes awards you extra balls with a special certficate.

You must clear a board of all orange pegs before advancing to the next one, and clearing all the levels lets you move up to new challenges. The game is for either solo players, or two in a duel mode in which you alternate turns.

There's no timing involved in the game; just judging the right bounce to clear the orange pegs.

TIP: Time shots where possible to have the moving pan catch a rebound, which earns you an extra ball or bounces the in-play ball back into the game board.

Sparkle HD ██

$4.99 • 10tons • http://5str.us/nqy

Shoot the orbs, earn amulets, and save the world

The framing story may seem a bit much at times—something to do with a wooded kingdom, a map, and amulets—but the gameplay is quite engrossing. Trails lead to a scepter of sorts at the center, which can fire gems. A snaking path of orbs tries to reach the scepter. Shoot out gems to build sets of three or more, which then vaporize.

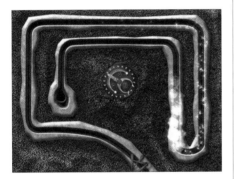

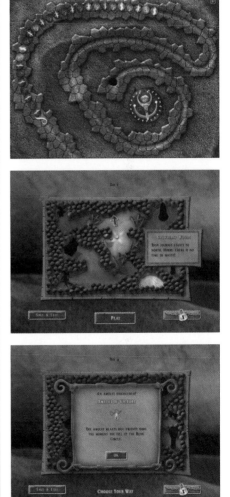

Special enhancements appear, which you shoot to claim, when you clear out multiple sequences of orbs. For instance, knock out three green spheres dividing more than three red ones, and you get a bonus as the matches cascade when sets join up in the gaps.

The higher the level you reach, the more amulets you unlock. Amulets add powers, such as blasting 20 orbs away at once. Gameplay increases in speed and quantity of orbs as you advance.

The game is reminiscent of Bejeweled (p. 55) without being beholden to it. You can set different modes of play, which make the game harder or easier.

The free version (iPad only) provides just the first several levels before encouraging an upgrade. Ignore the mythology and enjoy the sport.

MORE: Sparkle also comes in an iPod/iPhone version ($2.99, **http://5str.us/9v6**) and a free iPad release (http://5str.us/fv7)

The Incident

$1.99 • Big Bucket Software • http://5str.us/yqx

Take off your jacket and jump over objects piling up while grabbing ballons

Tilt, tap, tilt, tilt, tap, tilt, tap tap tap. The Incident makes two different game play elements collide: simplicity in controls with complexity in objects. Your little man in a tie, who removes his jacket at the game's outset, has to jump away from falling objects, and then on top of fallen ones.

Your goal is climb on ever-higher piles without getting smacked in the head too much or hit by skull-and-crossbones balloons, among other hazards.

Scramble up high enough, and you unlock new levels, each of which has a distinct background and theme from Street and City up to Orbit and Space. (In space, no one can hear you jump.)

Get smacked in the head too much, and you're toast, but you get an award based on the object that got you. Balloons with red crosses renew your vigor, while an occasional helmet falls your way to guard your noggin.

The objects that fall are hilarious. Everything from the everyday (sofas, cars, refrigerators, and TV sets) to the weird and sublime (René Magritte paintings, pediments from Greek architecture, and blocks of ice with a frozen guy inside). If your avatar gets stuck under a stack you can shake your device (top figure) to float your way out.

Like many games of this kind, you can never win, only persist.

NOTE: What's the incident that's referred to? I haven't reached the top. Perhaps in space, the answer is revealed. It's unclear if the game ever ends—and that's part of the mystery.

Angry Birds HD

$4.99 • Clickgamer Technologies • http://5str.us/ksh

Why can't angry birds and green, egg-stealing pigs get along?

Angry Birds is a silly, silly game involving ballistics, physics, angry birds, and green pigs. But it's quite fun and playable. The premise is ridiculous, of course. In a pre-game movie (and separately available film short), we see green pigs steal eggs from a set of birds. The birds vow revenge, extracted through many scenarios, each of which has its own bizarre animated opener.

Each level of Angry Birds comprises pigs under increasingly complicated edifices of lumber, glass, stone, and other materials, and birds that you slingshot in an arc to smash into said edifices to crumple them and destroy the pigs. (It's cartoon violence, and isn't gory.)

The basic red bird flies in a gravitationally accurate arc. As you ascend in levels, additional bird types are added among the munitions you must deploy, including ones that lay bomb-like eggs (or egg-like bombs), and a multi-bird that splits into three separate projectiles while tapped. Birds appear in a (sorry) pecking order: you have to fire them in the order they're queued.

The number of levels is astounding and expands regularly. You receive points for what you destroy and for penurious use of birds-as-weapons: bonus points are awarded for remaining birds. And even when you succeed in squashing pigs, success is ranked from one to three stars by points. This often shows you could be slightly more elegant in extracting sows' ears, encouraging you to try again.

If you miss but one pig on a level, it's not complete. Worse, the pigs smirk at you.

MORE: Both a limited free (**http://5str.us/iye**) and a full $0.99 (**http://5str.us/fdz**) version of Angry Birds are available for the iPhone/iPod touch.

Ramp Champ ▮▮▮

$1.99 • The Iconfactory • http://5str.us/mz3

It's like being on a constantly updated boardwalk

Skee ball is such an old-fashioned game to have modern appeal. But Ramp Champ has combined the silliness of rolling a ball to knock down things at the far end with the flexibility of the digital world. When you get bored with one layout or have mastered it, there are add-on packs to challenge you with new goals and scoring targets.

Ramp Champ comes with several themed levels. Each level starts with nine balls. Flick the balls so they leap up and hit targets. If you're particularly skilled, you can knock down two or more figures at once. A secret pattern of the correct items to knock down in each level adds more mystery.

I found in the Trick or Treat add-on pack that hitting the pumpkin repeatedly in combination with another target was the key to one goal. (That level also features a guest shot from Iconfactory chief Craig Hockenberry in vampire form.)

When you exhaust the balls, the game spits out tickets. Earn enough tickets and you can redeem them for virtual swag. Achievements are also rewarded with tiny trophies.

The folks behind Ramp Champ are die-hard Macheads, which you can tell from the Icon Garden level where you knock down famous Apple icons.

MORE: The game comes with three levels. Additional levels are sold in packs of three for 99¢ each as an in-app purchase. The North Pole is an exception as a single level pack.

Fruit Ninja

$0.99 • Halfbrick Studios • http://5str.us/r97

Slice fruit in half; the more at the same time, the better

Carmen Miranda might be in danger if surrounded by avid Fruit Ninja players. (Please raise your hand if you got that joke; otherwise, proceed to Wikipedia.)

This charming app scores you on how well you can continuously swipe your finger accurately to slice fruit in half as it's bounced up on screen.

Game play comes in three varieties. Classic can be played until you miss three pieces of fruit. Bombs are also interspersed with delectables: slice one and you're history.

A Zen mode is timed—a bit at odds with a reflective mood—but there are no bombs and no penalty for dropping fruit. My three-year-old son finds this particularly appealing; he aims for bananas.

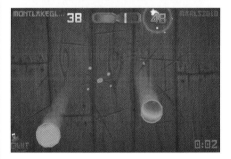

A multiplayer timed mode lets you match up via Game Center with friends or with any other interested player. A display shows the color of fruit you need to slice (blue or white). Slice the wrong fruit, and your opponent receives points.

All three modes offer bonuses for slicing three or more with one go.

After playing long enough and winning enough points, additional produce is added into the fruit salad. You also unlock weapons and backgrounds found via the Dojo link.

As a cute touch, to navigate among menus, you can't tap—you have to slice.

MORE: An iPad-only version of the game, Fruit Ninja HD, is also available (**http://5str.us/qks**).

Doodle Bowling Pro ■■

$1.99 • GameResort • http://5str.us/fbt

Ball beats paper

Doodle Bowling Pro combines the look of a sketchbook with the appeal of bowling. The game follows bowling rules, with your finger flicking to hurl the ball. You can give the ball some english by swiping up or down while it's in motion. The app scores the game like standard American bowling.

The doodle part of the name is belied by some of the 14 themes, which are more rendered than doodled. But they're all rather amusing, ranging from the mouth of hell to outer space to a rather conventional bowling alley appearance. Some include animation, which can be offputting or a challenge, depending on how well you concentrate.

The default theme for the app is quite gaudy (see below left), and you have to play games to unlock other themes.

While the game is sketchy, the physics are genuine. The ball interacts with the alley, and the pins with the ball and one

another, in an accurate and realistic fashion—as realistic as pencil drawings and three-dimensional renderings of the elements can be. Seven-ten splits are just as painful in the game as in real life.

The game hooks into Facebook to challenge friends, but you can also issue invites via email.

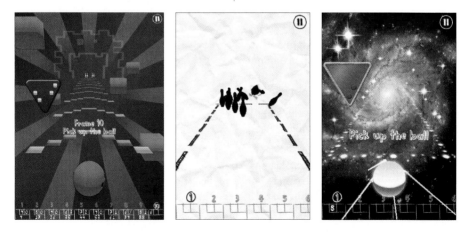

MORE: A free version with ads and lower-resolution graphics is also available (**http://5str.us/aha**).

Real Racing

$4.99 • Firemint • http://5str.us/qyq

Racing that makes your heart speed up, too

There's no game I've played on an iPhone that made my blood race quite as much as Real Racing. The app is a full-body experience, even though you're just tilting your iOS device and occasionally tapping on it.

Like all good road rally and racing games, you have a clear objective: be the fastest around a track. You have many choices on your path to racing supremecy, however.

The app offers the choice of several cars, with more available for unlocking as your skill level improves. Each car has particular attributes. You can adjust the assisted braking for each when you select one for a race. (The more assist, the less likely you are to spin off the track, but the less speed you can gain as a result).

To start in the game, you have to complete a qualifier in which you make it around a course in a minimum time. After that, you tap the Career button from the main menu to choose among courses. More courses are unlocked the longer and better you perform.

By default, you tilt your device to steer and tap or press the screen to brake. Acceleration automatically increases whenever you're not braking—or haven't just hit a wall or other obstacle. (There are no fiery explosions. You just have to steer yourself back on the track.) You can adjust the controls to several other settings, depending on what suits you.

The app simulates night and day, with sunlight poking you in the eyes during daytime races.

Real Racing lets you compete against nearby friends over Wi-Fi, or through ongoing online leagues you can join.

MORE: A free version sponsored by a carmaker with a single model is also available (**http://5str.us/f8n**).

Orbital

$2.99 • Bitforge • http://5str.us/1mf

Your knowledge of gravity comes in handy with this seemingly simple game

Orbital supposes that gravity warps space, and it's right. A gun of sorts sits at the bottom of the screen. Fire a ball of light, and, where it slows to a halt, it grows into a sphere bounded only by other spheres you've already created, and by the inside borders of the grid.

Knock another sphere with the new comet, and a number in the middle of the struck sphere counts down. The number indicates how many times a sphere must be struck by a projectile before disappearing in a blaze of rainbow light.

What's the challenge? Avoid bounceback across a line above the gun: stray one iota over that line and your game is over. The app zooms in dramatically for bounces that appear likely to cross.

The game requires patience and observation. A knowledge of billiards could help, as you bank shots.

You earn extra points for bounces that careen and take out more than one sphere in a shot. Compare points on a global leaderboard, and link to Facebook to share with friends. The high global scores show real dedication to the app.

In Gravity Mode, the grid distorts as you add spheres. Gravity pulls your projectile into the orbit of existing bodies, and slingshots the shot around. Aim correctly and you can skip bounces off a sphere, killing it with one shot.

Two other modes let you experiment with an Aristotolean universe (Pure Mode, in which gravity doesn't distort the grid), and Supernova Mode, where you fire a laser to point the direction you want a projectile to aim.

A two-player mode allows handing back and forth, and setting a best of *X* games to play: 1, 3, or 5. The free version only offers gravity mode up to 15 points.

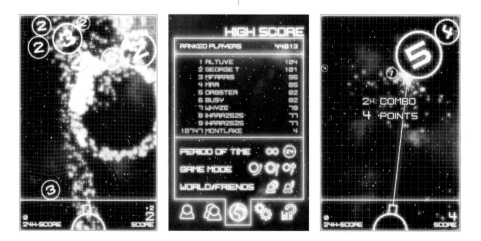

MORE: Orbital also comes in free (**http://5str.us/hvv**) and iPad versions ($2.99, **http://5str.us/gvl**).

Plants vs. Zombies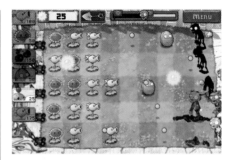

$2.99 • PopCap • http://5str.us/p5t

It's the oldest story in the book: weaponized plants fight the reanimated

Why can't plants and zombies get along? You got me. But apparently, PopCap discovered they're natural enemies, the quick and the not-so-dead.

Plants vs. Zombies is the sort of game that causes puzzled looks when you explain it to the uninitiated. Play takes place on a lawn, roof, or other arena, with plants on the left and zombies on the right. You're allotted some starting points, and accumulate more as you capture sunlight floating through the sky at regular intervals.

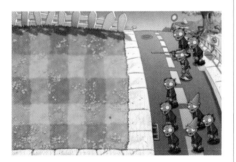

Points are exchanged for plants, which you place in a grid to fight back zombies. Some plants are useful, like the sun-flower, which is critical to replenishing your score. Plant a bunch of them to make more power-packing sun icons, but not so many that you disregard defending your actual turf.

Other plants fire peas or other pro-jectiles at zombies, gradually taking them down, while others just sit there waiting to be attacked. The more powerful a plant's function, like a set

of cherries that act like cherry bombs, the more expensive the item is in points. There are 49 kinds of plants.

The game's goal is to keep zombies from getting to the left side of the screen as they lurch into view. Zombies come with capabilities as varied as plants, some smarter or more tenacious than others. Pole-vaulting zombies run onto the field and jump over obstacles.

The game is silly—part of what makes it fun—while having a very focused and consistent set of elements. As you defeat hordes of the semi-living, you move up into new territory. PopCap built 50 layers of activity. The iPad includes even more options.

MORE: An iPad-only version with additional features, such as multitouch (several fingers at once) play, higher-res graphics, and an additional minigame, is also available ($9.99, **http://5str.us/gps**).

Chopper 2 ▐ ▮

$2.99 • Majic Jungle Software • http://5str.us/lkr

Fly a helicopter on rescue-and-destroy missions, tilting subtly to control flight

Chopper 2 is the most beautiful and subtle game I've ever played that involves my avatar killing people. The controls are fantastic, relying on the various sensors on an iPhone, iPod touch, or iPad to control the speed, height, and direction of a helicopter. The program takes advantage of the gyroscope included in newer iOS devices for finer control.

Your mission is to rescue civilians, defend the fellows on your side, kill enemy forces with laser-aimed weapons, and avoid hitting birds.

The tilt controls are very sensitive, but you master them over time. When firing weapons, the action becomes tricky: you must maintain the helicopter's position while tapping to aim and fire.

You work through 12 distinct locations, earning points along the way. A lovely 17-minute soundtrack accompanies the adventure.

The developer took the time to add an interesting feature—if you own the right set of two or more iOS devices. You can use an iPhone or iPod touch as a remote

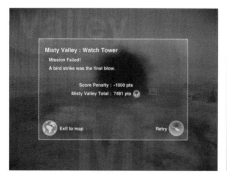

control for an iPad, iPhone 4, or 4th-generation iPod touch over Bluetooth or Wi-Fi. Even better, if you have a video output cable for the device that's being controlled, you can plug it into a television set or monitor.

MORE: The original Chopper is also available ($1.99, universal, **http://5str.us/jma**) as well as a free version with limited levels and low difficulty (universal, **http://5str.us/iue**).

Osmos HD ▮▪

$4.99 • Hemisphere Games • http://5str.us/xqa

Guide a cellular glob to release jets of fluid and absorb smaller entities

Osmos is a remarkable game. It looks and behaves like nothing I've seen before. It's compelling and beautiful. I'll try to explain why.

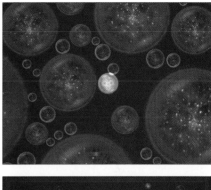

Your avatar in the game is a blue cell with a jellyfish-like pattern in the middle. You grow by absorbing smaller cell-like objects; the smaller the cell, the more blue it is. Larger objects are red, and can absorb you.

By tapping in the direction opposite where you want to move your globule, you emit small or large jets of your own substance. But as you emit bits of yourself, you shrink; and your jets can be absorbed by other cells. There's a fine tradeoff between locomotion and extinction.

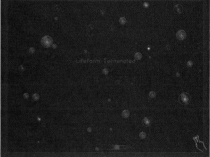

There are also "anti-matter" cells (colored green), which destroy an amount of red or blue cell components equal to themselves. Repulsing cells push back against you as you get closer.

Game play is divided at the top level into Odyssey and Arcade, although it's not clear what the difference is. Both have you achieve particular game goals.

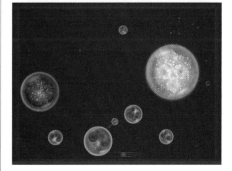

Odyssey sports level names like Nemocyte and Warped Chaos, while Arcade shows you a glimpse of the starting position. Arcade levels have increasing types of difficulty unlocked as you advance. Some levels start static, while others have fast-moving cells already bouncing around. You can make time flow more slowly or quickly.

It's hard to do justice to the oddness and beauty of Osmos, which carries a strong whiff of the ineffable, even as you're engaged in the play of the game.

MORE: Osmos is also available in an iPhone/iPod touch version ($2.99, **http://5str.us/lcn**).

Doodle Jump ▮▮

$0.99 • Lima Sky • http://5str.us/9dx

Among the most popular games, this app is hard to master, easy to enjoy

The strange trumpet-mouthed, armless creature that's your avatar in Doodle Jump leaps from doodle platform to doodle platform against a paper-grid background (with the occasional hole) as you tilt left and right. Miss a platform, and you plummet to your doom. The game is charming in its goofiness, but it's not unsophisticated.

As you rise ever higher, you encounter more enhancements and detriments. Monsters appear at random, making odd growling noises. Tap in the direction of the beast to fire the upward-facing shots out of your trumpet nose. You can also ignore them—just don't land on top of a plug ugly.

Platforms are typically stable, but some move back and forth, some are made of a material that crumbles when you jump on them, and others disappear.

To aid your trip upward, gifts have been left on various platforms. Hop on top to

take advantage of a spring, a trampoline, a jet pack, a propeller beanie, force fields, and more.

As you jump, you'll notice names and lines at the right, indicating the high score of someone else. Log into Facebook, and you can see friends' scores. Challenges are issued via email.

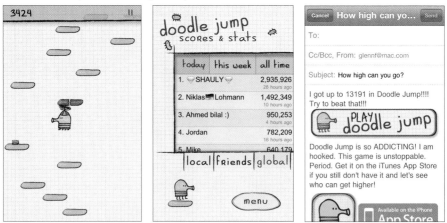

TIP: In the main menu, swipe left at the bottom of the screen (near the News label) to change the theme of the game. Several themes are available, from Christmas to jungle to outer space.

Canabalt ■■

$2.99 • Semi Secret Software • http://5str.us/nrn

If you don't jump, you fall. And watch for boxes and explosions

Canabalt is reminiscent of great eight-bit video games of the Atari era, but with the speed and controls of an iPhone. Canabalt requires continuous focus; it's not a casual game. The game is played entirely as a moving strip of action that scrolls from left to right.

You can't look away for a moment from the running man you control. You time jumps to leap gaps between one building and the next, avoid packing crates, and miss being squashed by stuff dropped from moving airships. Buildings also randomly collapse. Sometimes, you must time a leap to smash through a window into one floor of a building.

There's not much game control, but the time you hold down your finger corresponds roughly to the arc of the jump. Need to catch a breath? Tap pause, and take five.

The app sometimes vibrates your phone or other device to offer an advance warning about planes or rockets.

The background music can be changed, which is good as it becomes relentless. Tap in the upper-right corner on the main screen to cycle through three choices. The app recommends using headphones, and so do I: you'll drive everyone around you crazy otherwise.

It's very, very easy to die in his game, making the top scores more remarkable. 103,285 meters? That could be a few days of someone's time, with the pause button pressed between runs.

At the end, you die—a metaphor for life as a whole, perhaps? Your score is simply how far you ran in game meters before it was all over.

One could argue that most early arcade video games were "leaping" games. Not all involved actually jumping, although Mario is a prominent example. But the notion of moving ever higher was there.

Canabalt has stripped down those game elements to a more raw level than an arcade game ever dared. You run and leap, but mostly run. A tiny mistake, and you're gone. Scores aren't in points, but in persistence. The tip of the hat to those old games is obvious, but it's also subtle.

MORE: An iPad version is also available ($2.99, **http://5str.us/nrn**).

Fieldrunners

$2.99 • Subatomic Studios • http://5str.us/j1a

Blow up guys with an array of weapons before they reach safety

Fieldrunners could be an oddly considered game of financial modeling despite its shoot-'em-up nature. The tower-defense gameplay centers on placing ever more weapons in the correct fixed positions to shoot wave after wave of increasingly more resistant men and vehicles. You can also upgrade weapons after you first place them.

If 20 of either enemy makes it through your line of fire, you lose the round. Each round has 100 waves. Last for a full round and you unlock new levels; you can also adjust the level of difficulty.

You receive points in the form of dollars for every guy you wipe out or conveyance you destroy. These dollars buy you weapons, and purchase upgrades for weapons, until you have the ultimate version of that particular destroyer.

The more expensive the weapon, the more damage it inflicts. Choosing the right combination of rapid fire and quick discharge makes a difference in halting the onslaught. Weapons can be traded in (for considerably less) if you want to redeploy.

geoDefense Swarm

$1.99 • Critical Thought Games • http://5str.us/yjv

Honeycombed spaces must be defended

A swarm of creeps is crawling through hexagonally organized cells. Continually place and upgrade weapons to slow down and destroy the geometric shapes that are trying to reach the exit.

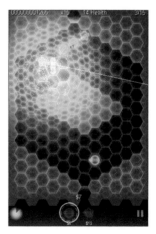

MORE: Fieldrunners is also available for the iPad ($7.99, **http://5str.us/rmi**). geoDefense Swarm is a successor to geoDefense, available in fee ($1.99, **http://5str.us/1rl**) and free (**http://5str.us/q8j**) versions.

6

Games of Strategy

Check your checkmate at the door, with games
of strategy that make you think before you move.
Strategy comes in many forms: ancient and classic,
trivial and perplexing—and the creation of life itself.

Deep Green Chess

$7.99 • Cocoa Stuff • http://5str.us/9d6

An enjoyable game of chess pitted against a merciless machine

I was smoked almost immediately, my lack of recent chess experience showing through. The power formerly reserved to desktop computers to perform deep analysis for a strong competitor is now in the palm of your hand.

Deep Green can play a straightforward game right out of the box, as it were. Fire up the app (you play white), make a move, and the computer responds. Tap a piece and then tap its destination, or drag a piece to an appropriate (and legal) square. It's all quite intuitive.

Underneath the game board are five buttons affecting play: new game (you're prompted to resign if a game is underway), revert a move (yours or the other player's), replay the last move, suggest a move, and view game settings.

Tap the i button, and you can change game options, pitting yourself against another human, or having two computer opponents fight it out. The computer

logic can be adjusted for how well it plays by limiting or expanding the amount of time from 1 second up to 30 seconds. There are also three tiers at 1 second in which the computer examines even fewer potential moves.

For advanced players, the Setup options let you place pieces in start-

ing positions on a board to observe or play a newspaper, book, or well-known game. You can also change castling options and other rules. Games can be replayed step-by-step on completion. (The game has only two missing elements: allowing multiple active gameboards, and storing completed games for later review.)

Deep Green Chess's roots are quite deep: the app dates back to the Apple Newton.

MORE: A free version is also available in which game play isn't restored from the point left off if you exit the app (http://5str.us/an2).

Strategery ▮▯

$1.99 • Affogato • http://5str.us/go4

A dice game of competing territories neatly digitized

The most engrossing games often arise from exceedingly simple rules, and such is the case with Strategery, a name borrowed from a George W. Bush parody by Will Ferrell. Strategery pits you against competing empire builders, each with territory comprising different-sized irregular hexagon shapes.

You fight to win more land by challenging adjacent property. The greater sum of a dice roll by the challenger or challenged makes the property shift hands. As you win more space, you acquire more dice (or "armies") based on your contiguous territory.

More dice make it easier to fight other competitors—but the dice guarantee you can't be assured of winning. And sometimes you don't want to throw a roll because you need a defense in the next round, keeping dice in reserve.

Game play can be set at varying levels of complexity, from easy to "brutal," and multiplayer games can be conducted online (with push notifications announcing updates) or in the same physical place using pass-and-play turns.

After a game, you can play the same board again (to learn from mistakes), or watch a replay to relive your agony.

Affogato maintains its own user registration system (at this writing), and you set up an account with them associated with your email addess (not exposed) and a username. You can issue challenges for multiplayer games by picking one of your contacts, entering a username, or asking for a random matchup against another Strategery user who has requested the same.

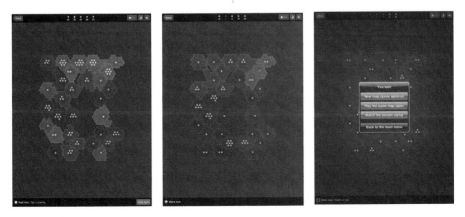

MORE: A free universal version is also available (**http://5str.us/1j9**) with full basic play but omitting some custom features and online multiplayer games.

FlightControl ▪▫

$0.99 • Firemint • http://5str.us/c97

Act as an air-traffic controller with your finger

I recall playing air-traffic controller (ATC) games when I was kid, using text-based terminal "graphics" (in which nothing used actual images), and later with primitive screen displays. Given how out-of-date ATC hardware was at the time, and still is, the experience was similar to the professionals and just as stressful.

FlightControl brings the ATC mindset without any of the charts, numbers, and other data. Planes and other flying vehicles come in from the borders of the screen, indicated by an a red circled exclamation point before they appear.

You swipe a path from the plane or helicopter to an allotted landing strip or landing pad (which lights up when you start to swipe). The path you draw msut allow the craft to ply the air while maintaining a minimum separation distance from other traffic. Whew.

The game features five airport layouts and 10 types of aircraft, and the developer promises more. You can hook up to land planes with friends (via Wi-Fi or Bluetooth), earn achievements, and share results via Game Center. A leaderboard shows results from nearby, too, if you allow your location to be shared

Some levels are harder than others. They aren't marked as such in the iPhone version. I crash planes into each other for the water-based aircraft carrier time and again.

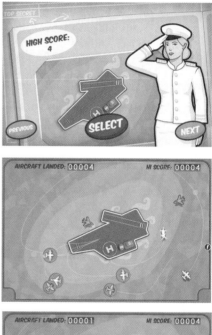

MORE: An iPad version, Flight Control HD, is also available ($4.99, **http://5str.us/dig**). The iPad version marks levels by difficulty.

Cat Physics

$0.99 • Donut Games • http://5str.us/ubl

Two cats, one ball, and the laws of physics

Cat Physics combines two things everyone loves: cats...and science! Ok, not everyone may love science (or cats), but if you're interested in trajectories and ballistics and enjoy the whimsy of having cats involved, this game is engrossing.

The premise is that two cats, in a cave-like landscape, are trying to pass a ball from one to the other using least distance to do so. (Some scenarios feature more than two cats as well as strange outdoor landscapes.)

The cats are typically separated by odd gulfs, overhangs, cliffs, and other obstacles. When the ball passes over any of a series of arrows scattered around the screen, it's propelled with a bit of thrust in the indicated direction.

Additional manipulators, like a spring-loaded pusher, appear in some levels. Sometimes obstacles are made of glass. Two kinds of rotors act to redirect action when a ball falls on them.

One particularly interesting challenge involves a set of undulating walls; timing is critical in those levels.

The game has 50 levels, and scores are based on the efficiency of your path for the ball compared to an optimum route known only to the game's designer. You score from one to three stars based on points, and can retry levels again and again, resetting arrows and other game components.

Doodle God ▮▮▮

$0.99 • JoyBits • http://5str.us/amm

Combine basic elements into ever more complex forms

Before the modern scientific method, many cultures believed that all material things comprised varying proportions of fundamental elements, like earth, water, fire, and air (and sometimes the ineffable aether or ether). Doodle God plays off this cultural history by offering you the chance to mix and match four starting elements to create (at this writing) 196 organisms.

You start with basic mixtures. Fire and water become lava. Sand and earth become clay. And so on. But you soon start reaching fascinating patterns, like plugging Life and Swamp together to get a living, moving creature. Mythical creatures can also easily result. I crossed fire with a bird and ended up with a phoenix; clay plus life brought me a golem.

This is no kingdom of life: some combinations are rather bizarre. Fortunately, a light bulb button at the bottom gives

you hints that may lead to the right conclusion. I was stumped at one point, until I was clued in that I could make coffee (seeds plus energy). A set of double light bulbs shows you the two categories that contain elements that might combine. After getting a hint, you have to wait a few minutes to get the next one.

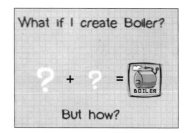

You can review a list of combinations you've made that turned into new elements. If you've connected up with Facebook, you can tap a row, and then tap a Facebook **f** to post the recipe to your Wall.

TIP: Your friends playing Doodle God might think you're giving them spoilers if you share too many recipes.

Qrank

FREE • Ricochet Labs • http://5str.us/5yd

Answer trivia questions while competing against the rest of the world

It's the ultimate bar trivia contest played on a global scale. With a new quiz each day, Qrank asks you to answer 15 questions drawn from a set of 20. Double and triple bonuses are hidden throughout. Questions are divided into easy, moderate, and hard, with more points awarded for more difficult questions. Each question is drawn from a category, like history or arts and entertainment.

You can use a magnifying glass tool to reveal the categories for one row; a set of pages when tapped shows the 2x and 3x bonuses in a single row you choose.

As you answer each question, you see your score compared to others playing simultaneously worldwide. Questions are insanely topical, sometimes based on news just a few hours old.

When the quiz is over, your city, state/region, country, and global range are shown. (I've been as high as 3,300 globally out of 6,000-odd players.)

You earn badges for playing well, fast, and frequently, and can share those badges over Facebook and Twitter.

The game lets you set up instant trivia contests at locations already defined on a map near you. You can also appoint a bar or restaurant as a new meet-up location. Five players are required to start these real-world games.

TIP: Did you know that China is the largest exporter of tungsten?

Blue Block ▪▪

$0.99 • Aragosoft • http://5str.us/7az

Slide a block and let the dragon escape the trap

Slide a block one way, then another. The dragon remains trapped. Look at the whole pattern to see how one move unlocks another, then another. It's maddening, fascinating and inescapable.

Blue Block is a spatial game with one rule and one goal. Blocks from one to five units long in a six-by-six grid may slide only in their longest direction: left and right, or up and down, and only one at a time, even if two blocks could move in the same direction. Moving blocks in enough ways releases the "dragon's block" which escapes through a gap to the right.

Depending on the version you use (free or paid), Blue Block has either thousands or tens of thousands of puzzles to unlock. After unlocking a puzzle, you can return to it to improve the number of moves it takes to solve. An iPad version (shown at upper right) has beautifully rendered game graphics.

Fortunately for my sanity (and yours), you choose the level of difficulty for puzzles from Kids through Expert and up to Crazy. I wasn't joking about sanity.

A successor game, Blue Block Double ($0.99, **http://5str.us/bwk**), requires manipulating blocks to release two blocks (below at far right).

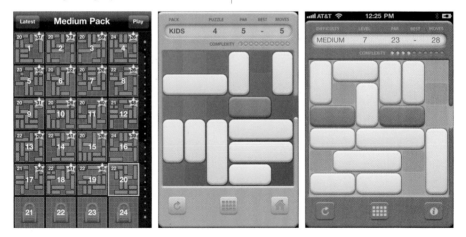

MORE: The game is available in original and two-block forms in many versions, including free. Free versions have substantially fewer puzzles. See all the apps by this developer at **http://5str.us/9cw**.

Labyrinth 2 HD ■■

$7.99 • Illusion Labs • http://5str.us/jdt

Old carved wooden balance game updated with pinball bumpers, cannons, and more

Labyrinth 2 HD is perhaps the apotheosis of tilt-and-balance games that mimic old-fashioned wooden mazes through which you must carefully thread a ball.

The digital advantage is that you can have thousands of different designs, and features that no wooden game could offer. This includes a button that, when crossed by the virtual ball, splits it into two smaller balls. Magnets, fans, bolts blocking entrances (with buttons to roll over to release them), and other elements are scattered throughout.

The gameplay also includes cannons, some of which fire balls that destroy your metal ones, while others fire shots that act as additional elements to avoid or bounce off.

If the huge number of levels included isn't enough to challenge you, Illusion Labs offers online iPhone/iPod touch and iPad level editors which you can use to create and save your own levels.

Labyrinth 2 HD also supports multiplayer games over Wi-Fi and Bluetooth with up to four players competing.

Labyrinth ■■

$2.99 • Codify • http://5str.us/bo9

Realistic portrayal of wood

For those who prefer the classic wooden labyrinth game with no extras, Labyrnth meets the mark (below, far right). Its 3D animation when tilted is lifelike, although it can be turned off for those who find it distracting.

The game includes over 1,000 levels, but you can create your own using a Web-based editor. Just enter a code from your phone, start creating a level, and download it. (A free version with 10 levels and ads is also available, **http://5str.us/1bd**.)

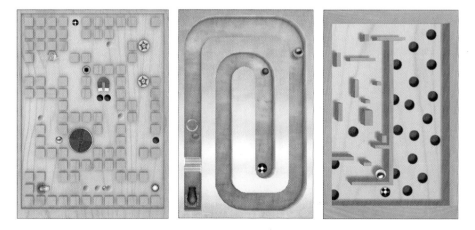

MORE: Labyrinth 2 also comes in two iPhone/iPod touch versions (free, **http://5str.us/5vb**) and paid ($4.99, **http://5str.us/3rh**), and a free iPad version (**http://5str.us/86z**).

7

Word Games

What's a seven-letter word for an ancient Greek vase? A ten-letter word that means "of or describing a random process"? If you know the answers,* this chapter's games should intrigue you. Your knowledge of language will serve you well as you are challenged to make words or come up with the right word to answer a question.

CROSSWORDS / JUMBLE / SCRABBLE / "SCRABBLE"

*Amphora and stochastic.

Scrabble for iPad

$9.99 • Electronic Arts • http://5str.us/rj8

A boardgame classic brought with superb extras to the virtual world

Scrabble isn't one of a kind any more; it has competition from other board and digital word games. However, it's an original and a classic, and the app version is an able conversion.

You can choose from several forms of game play, whether in the same room or with other players on the Internet. A pass-and-play ("Pass'N Play"!) mode lets you hand an iOS device around to let each person take his or her turn while hiding the tile rack from other players.

The app lets you match up with Facebook friends after logging into that service. You can also join or offer public games with other Facebook users looking for a match. A separate Tile Rack app for the iPhone or iPod touch (free) lets you put an iPad in the middle as the game board, using your smaller device to handle your game play.

Scrabble manages up to 25 games at a time. You can also pit yourself against the computer at varying levels of expertise each of which limits the size of the word list the computer consults.

A shuffle option rotates your letters through random combinations, which can sometimes stimulate the little grey cells to come up with a new idea.

If you need a little help finding or verifying words, an in-game official dictionary lets you type in words to test them (but not scan through them), and shows a list of all legal two-letter words. A hint feature will dig up the best word you can play up to four times per game.

After each turn, a board is updated at the top of the screen with each round's word and score. It offers a way to figure out how your scorned opponent managed to get 76 points with a three-letter play involving Q, Y, and Z.

MORE: While the iPad is an expansive way to play Scrabble, the game is also available for the small screens of the iPhone and iPod touch ($2.99, **http://5str.us/2tu**). Scrabble Tile Rack is free (**http://5str.us/9t5**).

Words with Friends

$2.99 • Newtoy • http://5str.us/g6r

It's like chess by mail for the always-connected age

Words with Friends lets you play a quite familiar word game (*cough*, 🆂🅲🆁🅰🅱🅱🅻🅴, *cough*) with friends in a turn-by-turn approach that allows up to 20 simultaneous games to be conducted over a local network or the Internet. A separate chat follows each game, too, to let you taunt or whine at your partner.

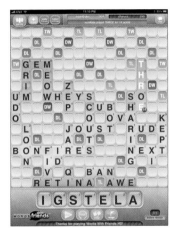

For players in the same place, you can use a pass-and-play mode in which turns alternate, and the letter rack shows only the current player's tiles during his or her turn. Moves are signaled via push notifications.

Perhaps trying to avoid criticism from Scrabble's makers, the board puts words score bonuses in different places. This takes a little getting used to.

When you place a word and tap Submit, you're blocked if any of the words formed aren't in the standard dictionary.

The game lets you set up an account directly with the developer, and find other registered friends using their in-game moniker. You can also contact friends on Twitter and Facebook, although you're not assured they own the app.

If you don't have pals, buddies, or tweeters ready to play, the Random Opponent option tries to match you up with someone else who wants a game.

The folks at Newtoy have a good sense of humor: the company released a free version of this app called Words with Pirates (**http://5str.us/rdu**) for international Talk Like a Pirate Day. All the words in that version be *grrr!* and *arrr!*

MORE: Words with Friends comes in a paid iPhone/iPod version ($2.99, **http://5str.us/t6f**) and a free, ad-supported version for the iPhone/iPod touch (**http://5str.us/n62**).

2 Across

$5.99 • Eliza Block • http://5str.us/zx5

Find puzzles from many sources, and solve them

2 Across is a solid offering that provides access to over two dozen sources of puzzles, including *The Houston Chronicle*, *The Onion*, and *The Wall Street Journal*. You can solve puzzles by showing clues in a variety of ways, including a view that lets you scan through them.

After choosing a source, scroll through a wheel by date and year to find puzzles. You can download one by tapping Download, or tap Add to Queue to set up multiple items to download at once.

Tap on a square on the grid to start solving. You can swap among Grid, Clues, and Split views to choose how you work through solutions.

A cheat mode—the developer's word, not my description!—offers the option to check whether a letter, word, or the whole puzzle is right; it can be turned off. You can also reveal a letter, word, or the whole dang puzzle (select Reveal

and Grid, then tap Reveal Grid when and if you get fed up).

The app provides access to New York Times Premium crosswords for subscribers to that service, too.

Crosswords ▮▮

$9.99 • Stand Alone • http://5str.us/vda

Cruciverbalists rejoice: gain access to a huge array of current and past puzzles

Crosswords provides access to over two dozen crossword sources, mostly newspapers, and lets you access premium accounts you may have at those sources. The app provides a comfortable interface for tapping in your answers.

Select a puzzle, and it appears with clues on one side in the iPad version and in landscape mode on an iPhone/iPod touch. In portrait mode on the smaller iOS devices clues are shown one at a time below the puzzle or in a separate tab. (In landscape mode, no tabs are shown; rotate to portrait to view tabs, change settings, or switch puzzles.)

Tap a square on the puzzle, and the appropriate clue for across is highlighted or shown. Double-tap the clue to swap between across and down. As you type, letters fill the squares, skipping those already filled unless you tap directly on such square.

The makers of the app provide a variety of hints (read "cheats"). On the iPhone/iPod touch, a Hints button appears at the top of the Across and Down clues list; on

the iPad, hold down on a square. You can check a letter or word, or reveal a letter, clue, or the puzzle. There's also a link to clue suggestions at OneAcross.com.

A pencil/pen tool switches between entering letters in gray or black. You can also enter up to 10 letters in a square (iPad only) to test out solutions.

Those who have a competitive streak may like the time clock (optional), and the ability to post how fast you solved a puzzle to a leaderboard run by the company, and to Twitter and Facebook.

MORE: A light version is also available (universal, **http://5str.us/ww2**)

Moxie ▪▫

$0.99 • Blue Ox Technologies • http://5str.us/yet

Fill in the squares to make words as letters appear, but don't make twaddle!

Moxie relies heavily on an extensive personal knowledge of words of five or fewer letters. Moxie shows you three rows of five blanks. In a round, a letter appears at right, and you tap a blank to fill it and make a word.

Moxie 2 (landscape figures at right) bumps that up to six letters, which makes it possible to rack up higher scores, but also adds to the challenge in finding words that fit in successive rounds.

As you create legitimate words—or words that the apps recognize, at least—points float over the screen. Fail to make a word and you're punished with points off and the label "twaddle!" floating by. Skip letters you can't fit by tapping Pass, rather than score a penalty.

Moxie and Moxie 2 score by adding together the point value of the letters in a word and then multiplying those points by the word's length.

You receive extra points for composing the current Moxie words based on a category you choose, such as animal or vegetable. There's also a daily set of challenge words.

High scores can be uploaded globally and compared for bragging rights.

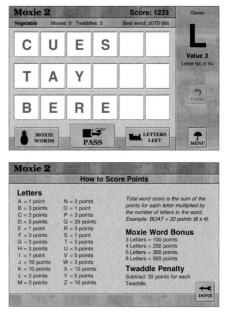

MORE: Moxie also has a free version (**http://5str.us/hu9**); Moxie 2 comes in free (**http://5str.us/8kl**) and fee ($0.99, **http://5str.us/7m8**) versions.

Jumbline

$0.99 • Brainium Studios • http://5str.us/b1m

Word-scrambling puzzle leaves you panting to fill in blanks

Jumbline forces you to think fast. You sort through letters to creates words of varying lengths before time's up. It's like Scrabble without intersecting words.

You set parameters for a game, such as how many letters you're given (5, 6, or 7) and how long you have (which affects bonus points).

When play starts, you drag letters to form words and swipe underneath a set when you get a match. Legitimate words populate empty lines to fill a game board. It requires the word-depth knowledge of Scrabble, to be sure, while the time limit (which can be set to "infinity") keeps things interesting.

As you play, you unlock badges, and can link into Facebook to trumpet success. This also lets you compare yourself to friends and a global leaderboard.

Jumbline 2 for iPad

$2.99 • Brainium Studios • http://5str.us/9ik)iPad

Shoot down clouds of words while building towers into the sky

Jumbline 2 adds two additional word-sorting games: a cloud mode, in which you tap clouds and form one word from the letters before the clouds exit the screen; and Star Tower, which requires you to build words rapidly, one on top of another.

Jumbline 2 is available in three other versions: free and paid versions for the iPhone/iPod touch and a free iPad version. The free versions have ads and only show shorter words, as does a free version of regular Jumbline.

MORE: The links! Jumbline Lite (free, **http://5str.us/akh**); Jumbline 2 for iPhone/iPod: free (**http://5str. us/i3y**), $1.99 (**http://5str.us/3i5**); Jumbline 2 for iPad: free (**http://5str.us/yh7**).

8

For the Kids

Whether you want to teach, entertain, or distract your kids, there are apps. Whether reading, learning, tapping, or decorating, kids already intuitively know how to use the device. Just make sure it doesn't drop!

Pickin' Time ▮▯

$0.99 • The Iconfactory • http://5str.us/7wv

Tap a fruit or vegetable, and more and more appear ever smaller

Pickin' Time is about the perfect small kids' app, although my three year old and six year old seem to like it equally well. Beautifully drawn fruits and vegetables appear during the timed game, and you tap the right bit of produce to add to your total.

The game can be played in single or multi-player mode. In the former, you tap to cycle through a potential avatar, like a tomato, zucchini, strawberry, or onion, and then begin to play. Items appears against a background that gradually changes from yellow to red as time runs out. The time remaining is shown along the bottom of the screen.

The fruit or vegetable you or your smaller compatriot picked appears alongside others. Tap to select it. Tap incorrectly and something like a

game-show buzzer for a wrong answer sounds. My littler one (shown left) sometimes plays to lose because the sound is so hilarious.

If you wait too long before tapping, a giant blue arrow appears and animatedly points at the right choice alongside the text, "Pick this one!"

Each time the correct item is chosen, the next set that appears includes more bits of produce to make it harder to tap it the next time. Score too quickly and you have a screen of dozens of rotating farmers' market candidates.

At the end of a single-player game, the number of items you picked tumbles

TIP: When the edibles pile up on the screen at the end of a single-player game, you can slosh them around by tilting your device.

onto the screen as the count is shown. Tilt the device, and the biomass shifts around for post-game hilarity.

The multi-player mode is also a hoot. Select multiplayer, and you can either have everyone crowd around one device (an iPad might be appropriate here) or connect via Wi-Fi to other iOS devices running Pickin' Time. In Wi-Fi mode, one device acts as a host and up to three others can join it.

When sharing a device, everyone chooses a distinct plant product and only taps when it appears. The fastest player wins based on the accumulated time for all of his or her picks.

When using multiple devices, each user picks a fruit or vegetable on the mobile device in their hands. During the game, you only tap when the right item shows up on your screen. The fastest player wins in that mode, too.

Talking Carl

$0.99 • Awyse •
http://5str.us/3ec

I'm just repeating what you're saying

A bit of fluff and nonsense you may say, but Talking Carl provokes peals of laughter from people of all ages. Carl doesn't do much but repeat what you see in a funny, higher-pitched voice. When you laugh, he laughs. You can also poke, pinch, and tickle Carl, and he reacts.

For your best enjoyment of this app, find a small child (see my older, below), don't explain it to him or her, and see what happens. You can also pit Carl on two devices against himself.

WARNING: Do not taunt happy fun Carl (http://5str.us/cre).

Cupcakes ▮▮

$0.99 • Maverick Software • http://5str.us/u3u

Let your kid enjoy as many cupcakes as he or she wants with no mess

If you have or had a small child in your life, you know the fidgets hit whenever he or she or they are forced to wait. Cupcakes is a great app for keep the fidgets at bay by exploring creativity—and wasting time, and enjoying all of the above.

You can use the simulation to aid in teaching how to bake later, even following a decoration recipe that the app can produce and share.

Cupcakes takes you through the process of making and decorating cupcakes. Start by choosing cupcake baking paper, followed by batter for a tray of four.

The cupcakes are baked in an oven for the time you choose. Don't be fooled by the "60-minute" timer—60 minutes takes about five seconds. The longer you put the cupcakes in for, the darker they become. Don't get burned! (See the Cajun-blackened cupcakes above right.)

Touch cupcakes or shake phone to get the cupcakes out of the pan!

After baking the cupcakes, you shake them out, and then decorate. The number of decorations possible is quite overwhelming. The "overchoice" might paralyze some kids—it nearly did me. You choose among frosting, toppings, branded jelly beans, and candy letters. Each of those categories has a huge

MORE: An iPad-only version is also available as Cupcakes XL ($0.99, **http://5str.us/col**).
WARNING: Do not let your child eat your iPhone.

Appscake

Fill a white liner with chocolate cake batter

Bake for 10 minutes

Add toppings: letter a, letter p, letter s, maraschino cherries, candy corn
Add Jelly Belly® jelly beans: berry blue, blueberry

number of options. A little one could spend a good hour just decorating.

Once decorated, a cupcake can be put in the fridge as a cupcake copy, shared (including the "recipe" for making it), or eaten. Complete cupcakes can also be emailed as a photo, saved to the Photo Library, uploaded to Facebook, or submitted to a Hall of Fame. The cupcake at right was sent to me by my children.

In the eating stage, you can add a filling that appears as bites are taken, or put candles on top which can be extinguished by blowing into the mic or shaking the device. Silly and marvelous.

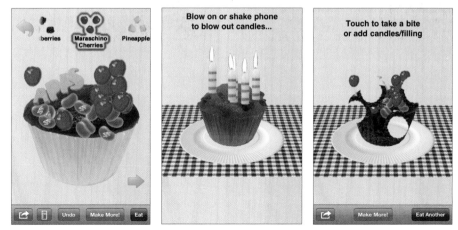

SUGAR HIGH: If all this frosting is sending you up the wall, try the company's other apps, including More Salad! and More Pizza! (Also, More Cowbell.) See **http://5str.us/esc**.

MathBoard ▋▊▪

$3.99 • Palasoftware • http://5str.us/wti

An entertaining way to drill math problems with selectable complexity

Arithmetic drills can be tedious, but they remain the foundation of lifelong mathematical knowledge and ability. MathBoard at least makes them well-presented, fun challenges. The iPad app emulates a chalkboard, which may mystify children who have never seen one.

The software lets you choose among seven operations. They include the familiar addition, subtraction, multiplication, and division. But you and your children will be challenged by squares, cubes, and square roots. These advanced operators stretch the program from elementary school to far beyond.

You can set limits to avoid frustration or increase the challenge for yourself and others. For instance, you can set the total number of problems to solve in a set, or adjust the range of numbers to avoid problems that include values that are beyond the mathematical scope of the person using the program. A 1st

grader might be taken aback at being asked to multiply 43×107.

While solving problems, a work area on the chalkboard appears at the bottom—and can expand full screen—with multiple colors of chalk.

There's also a built-in "problem solver." This tool walks you through solving an equation, showing each step along the way. This helps reduce the complexity of a problem to its component pieces.

The app has charm without losing track of its fundamental purpose. Maybe it will spur an interest in actual slates—they're highly portable and never crash!

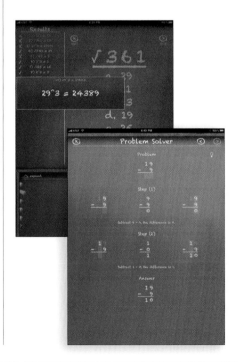

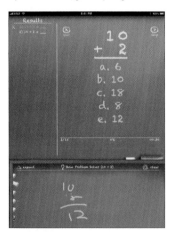

MORE: A free version, MathBoard Addition, limited to sums, is available (**http://5str.us/86r**). The software makers also offer SpellBoard ($4.99, **http://5str.us/8mb**) for spelling drills.

The Cat in the Hat ▪▫

$3.99 • Oceanhouse Media • http://5str.us/d2u

The whimsy of the book is preserved for young readers and all listeners

My three year old, Rex, sat next to me, transfixed. He'd heard *The Cat in the Hat* by Dr. Seuss before, but never quite in this format. On the iPad, the book was reading to him, zooming in and out on the pictures slowly as the story unfolded.

He could tap any object on screen, and its name would appear in overlaid type while the word or words were spoken, often in an appropriate character voice. A little swipe, and we advanced to the next page.

The app can be used more like a book, too, in which pictures and words appear, and you or your young reader gives voice to them. Tap the text in this mode, and it's spoken. Each word turns red as it is said aloud.

I commend the less-is-more approach of the app developers, similar to some of the best "videos" of books where images from the story are slowly enlarged and then remain static, rather than being full of extraneous motion.

The book's graphics were scanned at extremely high resolution, revealing the great art of Ted Geisel, as well as his terrific text.

MORE: An absopazoozle of other Dr. Seuss books are available in the App Store, many in universal form; many cost less (**http://5str.us/qhi**). Pictured at bottom right, *Hop on Pop* (**http://5str.us/foc**).

Itsy Bitsy Spider

$0.99 • Duck Duck Moose • http://5str.us/eku

Even though we know how the story ends, the tale's worth telling again and again

Duck Duck Moose makes great apps for kids. My favorite—mostly because it's my kids' favorite—is Itsy Bitsy Spider. The app sports beautifully-drawn colorful imagery, and it plays the familiar song about the indefatigable spider. What makes it wonderful is simple: tap on anything to make something happen.

Sure, you can (and should) tap on the spider itself. That advances it to another of the app's four panels, and sings the next line of the song. But tapping everywhere else produces fun outcomes and adds to the app's appeal.

Tap on a window, and a random animal might fly out, complete with silly sound effect. Tap again, and a new one appears. As the spider progresses on his journey up the waterspout, you'll occasionally encounter colorful eggs. Tap them, and they'll land on the spider's head. Collect enough and, at the apex of his journey, create a rainbow.

These literal Easter eggs are easy for children to discover, and mine figured them out quickly. You can turn a caterpillar into a butterfly, stack hats from flying birds onto the spider's head, and more.

As in most Duck Duck Moose apps, you can change the music to a simple orchestration or another language. Even better, you can record yourself—and your kids—singing the tune, too.

MORE: An iPad version of Itsy Bitsy Spider is also available ($1.99, **http://5str.us/bjb**)

Tozzle

$1.99 • Nodeflexion • http://5str.us/lhb

Puzzles to occupy the curious toddler

My kids wake up too early. When daddy's not ready to open his eyes all the way and the young ones are clamoring for attention, Tozzle can score me an extra half hour of shuteye.

The game offers more than 30 colorful puzzles. New pieces to fit into the puzzle are presented one at a time, and you (or more likely, your toddler) simply drags the object and drops it into position. Every puzzle piece you place triggers a silly sound effect or cheer.

If you can't figure out where to position a tough piece, Tozzle eventually shows an arrow to guide you in the right direction.

Puzzles become interactive once you solve them: the musical instrument or virtual machine you've assembled can be played or operated.

A cleverly implemented dragging mechanism prevents kids from dismissing the puzzle they're working on accidentally. That's not to say one clever youngster couldn't figure out how to do it—intentionally!—when ready to switch to a new puzzle.

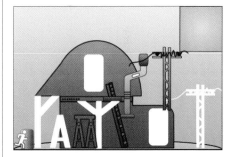

The puzzles range in difficulty. Easier ones feature a few big animal shapes or letters, while more complex ones require dozens of pieces—some of them quite small. The puzzle pieces are perfectly suited for kids' tiny fingers.

As an added bonus, the game should boost shape recognition and fine motor skills. But the most important part is simple: it's pretty darn fun.

A free version features just a small handful of puzzles, but is otherwise identical.

While Tozzle is an iPhone/iPod touch-optimized game, it looks just fine double-sized on my iPad, like many kids' games.

MORE: A free version of Tozzle includes fewer puzzles (**http://5str.us/pou**).

9
Video

The iPad didn't kill the television; it just shifted it around. Video streaming apps in this chapter work on the iPad, iPhone, and iPod touch, and finally bring us closer to having univeral playback of media wherever we are. Also, create, edit, and upload from a phone. It's the future!

STREAMING / PROGRAMS / EDITING

Hulu Plus ▮▪

FREE* • Hulu • http://5str.us/fit

Network television and more wherever you go

Hulu.com launched with a splash: Get broadcast television programs at standard-definition quality streamed over the Internet to your computer. The cost? Watching ads—but not nearly as many as on TV. (A Hulu hour has a few minutes of ads, which compares to 15–20 for cable and broadcast.)

But Hulu had a few weaknesses. New shows are broadcast over the airwaves (remember those?) at high-definition quality, and similar HD quality shows can be downloaded for a price from the iTunes Store and other digital stores. Further, many programs were available only in snippets, and complete episodes were only available for a few weeks.

Hulu Plus tries to bridge that gap. For $9.99 per month, the service brings streaming HD-quality programs for a show's current season and adds complete archived past seasons. You still have to watch ads, but that's part of the deal to avoid more complicated, illegal, or expensive ways to obtain the same programming.

The Hulu Plus universal app is part of the service. Subscribers can also stream standard and HD video to a browser on a Mac or Windows computer.

Your Hulu subscriptions (programs you track) and queue (new episodes of those programs) are a tap or two away. You can browse for programs and add them to your queue, as well as browse and watch immediately.

Subscriptions are invitiation only as I write this, but Hulu Plus is expected to go into wide release by 2011.

ACCOUNT: *The app requires a $9.99-per-month subscription to the Hulu Plus service. The subscription provides access from all your devices and computers, and includes streamed HD content to computers.

Netflix ■■

FREE* • Netflix • http://5str.us/geb

View movies anywhere from Netflix's streaming collection

Netflix has tens of thousands of movies and television shows available for instant streaming to its subscribers. The Netflix app brings your account and access to any iOS device, so long as a network connection is available.

You can see your instant queue, and add new items to it, as well as pick up at the point you left off in movies that you started viewing elsewhere.

The app automatically reduces bandwidth use over a 3G network, but you can still burn up a considerable amount, as much as 250 MB an hour. Over Wi-Fi networks, there's no app-based bandwidth limit (watch for specific hotspot or home broadband caps on usage) and the quality is generally better, but that depends on the Internet connection.

The iPad appearance of this app has the worst interface of any included in this book. It's merely the company's Web site, which works in the app erratically

and slowly. There's no queue management or other useful account features. The iPod/iPhone flavor isn't beautiful, but organizes results in a simpler and faster-to-navigate fashion.

Netflix makes the cut because of the sheer fun of having its streaming library available from any iOS 4 device. The company clearly needs to make the iPad flavor of the app behave more like an an iOS program—but I'd rather have it in this form than not at all.

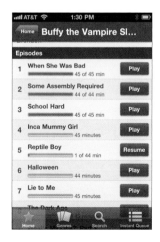

ACCOUNT: *Requires a Netflix DVD-by-mail subscription of at least $8.99, which includes unlimited streaming and one disc out at a time. (A cheaper limited streaming plan is excluded from iOS app viewing.)

Air Video

$2.99 • inMethod • http://5str.us/h5r

Stream video from computers on the local network without converting

Air Video has a simple purpose: to give you access to video stored on computers, whether a dedicated home-entertainment system or other computers you use for ordinary purposes. Free Mac OS X (10.5+) and Windows (XP, Vista, 7) server software is available.

Each computer that you set up with access software needs to be configured to point to folders containing the video you want to watch remotely.

The server can also be set up to convert video to a specified resolution and quality, which can reduce or expand bandwidth requirements. (Smaller files will stream better, but the video quality will be poorer, too.)

In the app, you connect to a server on the local network, and can browse the folders that were set up on that machine. There's an option in the server software to provide access over the Internet, too. Watch your 3G bills!

Select a video to play. If it's in a format that iOS can play without conversion, you can stream the original file immediately. You can also choose to convert the file to reduce the file's size for better use over the network.

For other formats, you can choose to convert (which puts the file into a queue), or play with live conversion. Live conversion quality depends on the file's original resolution and the power in your computer's processor. A slower machine can cause hiccups in playback.

MORE: You can try out Air Video using Air Video Free (**http://5str.us/2c9**), which works the same, but only shows you a few items per folder on a server.

ZumoCast ■▪

FREE* • Zector • http://5str.us/km2

All your media on all your machines available everywhere

ZumoCast gives you access to all the movies and audio you have stored on all your computers. One ZumoCast account makes this media available to you over a local network or the Internet via this app or a Web browser.

To make this all work, you start by setting up a free account at ZumoCast. You then install a small, free server package on as many computers you like. The software is available for Windows and Mac OS X. On each computer enter your ZumoCast account information, and use a folder organizer to link in your directories that contain media.

After setting up the computers, all their content is browsable and streamable through the ZumoCast app or on properly equipped desktop Web browsers

ZumoCast "transcodes" the content, or converts it from one format to another while it plays. iOS devices can only play certain video formats, and the rest need to be converted, which can be tedious and time consuming. ZumoCast's transcoding turns most video formats into iOS-compatible streams.

ZumoCast is divided into Files, Music, and Video. The software recognizes music and video type and builds a catalog from which you can select. Files shows the raw contents of the folders on a given computer.

The system picks up as much organization from the original as it can, showing music in albums and videos in folders.

MORE: The firm also makes ZumoDrive for access to Internet-based storage (1–2 GB free, **http://5str.us/8yc**).
ACCOUNT: *Requires free ZumoCast account.

iMovie ██▪

$4.99 • Apple • http://5str.us/zct

Edit movies and share them from an iPhone 4 or newest iPod touch

Apple included primitive video-trimming features when it added video capture to the iPhone 3GS model. The iMovie app goes several steps further, allowing you to trim, combine, and transition between clips, as well as put a frame with a label in one of several included styles.

Now, iMovie for the desktop it ain't, although it is impressive. You can't apply text where you want, only on the theme frame and only in a specified area. Transitions are limited, and trimming can be tedious, involving a lot of scrolling and dragging.

But if you're regularly shooting video on your iPhone 4 or 4th-generation iPod touch, iMovie is a remarkable tool to quickly produce something attractive.

Start by tapping the + sign in the upper right, which creates a new project. Select a theme, which is used for the opening of the video. Tap the down arrow to add video, still photos, and audio.

Video clips and photos can have audio enabled or not, be split or trimmed, and have title text placed on top. Pinch and expand a clip to space out or shrink the time interval displayed. Tap a clip to move the playhead (a vertical red line) where you want, and then swipe down to split the clip.

You can preview at any time by tapping the play button, or add video by tapping the camera button. Tap the gray box between any two clips to add transitions, like a cross dissolve, or your theme.

When you've assembled your masterpiece, export in 360p, 540p, or 720p (HD) formats to your Camera Roll. To move the video out, switch to Photos to upload or transfer (email, MMS, MobileMe, or YouTube), use USB to sync to iPhoto, or employ Dropbox (p. 171) to move to its storage system.

10

Messaging & Voice

This chapter's unofficial subtitle? How to beat the high cost of calling. And texting. And beat phone company pricing altogether. The apps in this chapter let you work around limitations in cell calling plans, message with friends and colleagues, and wind up none the poorer for the experience.

Skype

FREE* • Skype Software • http://5str.us/n6v

Free high-quality Internet phone calls and text chat worldwide with no fuss

Skype made its reputation by letting people talk to each other at no cost and with high voice quality over the Internet using its free software. The Skype app took a few revisions, along with changes to Apple's iOS, before it brought the same level of ease and access to mobile devices. A few pieces are still missing.

Skype's desktop software offers audio, video, and text chat between Skype users, as well as screen sharing. For extra fees, you can place and receive calls from the regular phone network, have a voicemail box, and send text messages worldwide.

The iOS app incorporates most—but not all—of those features: it can handle audio calls and audio chat, as well as text chat and text messaging. Video and screen sharing aren't available yet. You set up features on Skype's Web site, such as an inbound phone number, and

those features are then available in the iOS app. (Text messaging involves a per-message fee, as in the desktop version.)

Tens of millions of people already use Skype, and you can place direct calls from this app to them. There's no calling plan required and no per-minute fees.

You can use Skype credits to call regular phone numbers anywhere in the world, which are charged at Skype's low metered rates. If you buy an inbound phone number, this app can receive calls from the public phone network.

iOS 4 can notify you about incoming calls when Skype isn't active, so long as you signed in to Skype the last time you used it. You can also exit Skype when a call is in progress without losing the call.

Skype includes support for voice and text chat over 3G, not just over Wi-Fi. Skype audio consumes little bandwidth.

ACCOUNT: *Requires free account. Paid upgrades and per-minute calling rates are also available.

Line2 ▮▮▮

FREE* • Toktumi • http://5str.us/21e

A replacement for voice calling on an iPhone or any iOS device

People often complain about the high cost of cellular voice and text-messaging plans relative to the cost of data on the same plan. And that's a legitimate complaint. Even with the cost of AT&T and international carriers' metered 3G service for iPhones and 3G iPads, you still pay several cents a minute for cellular calls that would be the equivalent of a penny or less for an Internet call.

Toktumi seems to have figured out a middle ground between pure VoIP services like Skype and pure calling services offered by cell companies. This option could save quite a bit without any apparent sacrifice.

The firm's Line2 app and service provides unlimited calling and text messaging to U.S. and Canadian numbers, as well as voicemail and a variety of call features. You get a "real" phone number, too, with the state and area you choose.

Line2 works well with the latest iOS 4 features: even when the program isn't running, incoming calls prompt push notifications you can use to answer. If

a regular cell call comes while you're talking over Line2, you can shunt the cell caller to voicemail and resume your Line2 conversation. The software works over both 3G and Wi-Fi. 3G VoIP is initially turned off, as you could rack up cell data fees on limited plans.

Toktumi offers text messaging just like a cell company. This means no compromises about with which other networks you can exchange messages, and no charges for such messages.

Calls outside the U.S. and Canada are charged at relatively low international rates—extremely low compared to the ridiculous prices cell carriers levy.

Line2 also lets you use your cellular connection to handle its calls when, say, the data connection is poor. This keeps the cost of international calls low, and makes sense on evenings and weekends when many cell plans don't meter voice.

ACCOUNT: *A Toktumi account is required for use. After a 30-day free period, Toktumi costs $9.95 per month or $49.95 for six months. A $14.95-per-month account adds computer-based calling and advanced calling features.

BeejiveIM ▆▊▊

$9.99 • Beejive • http://5str.us/43d

Chat on all your favorite instant messaging services from a single app

BeejiveIM answers the question of how to cope with proliferating instant-messaging (IM) software. The app lets you enter multiple accounts from any supported services, which include AIM (AOL Instant Messenger)/Apple MobileMe, Facebook, Google Talk, Jabber servers, MySpace, Windows Live Messenger, and Yahoo Messenger.

After setting up accounts, you can log in or out of all of them at once, and set the same status message across all of them. With push notifications turned on, BeejiveIM alerts you to new IMs even if it's not the app you're running.

Buddies from every service are unified into single entries, even if they have multiple accounts at a single chat system. Icons next to their names identify the instant-message networks to which they're connected. Online status and status messages are shown. Group chats are supported on several services.

The app makes it easier to switch among active chats, send photos (either a picture you take or an image from your library), and record audio. You can even tap a mail icon to ship off a transcript of the chat to the other party.

BeejiveIM can also use AIM or Yahoo to send out text messages (SMS) over the cell network.

MORE: An iPad-only version is also available (BeejiveIM for iPad, $9.99, **http://5str.us/vjk**).

Textie Messaging ▮▮▮

FREE* • Borange • http://5str.us/oti

How to beat the high cost of texting

Textie Messaging bypasses the ridiculous cost of text-messaging systems by not using them. Borange has built its own server systems that pass messages among Textie users, storing and forwarding them—cheaply for them, and no cost at all to you.

Textie is free but sports ads; you can pay $1.99 to remove them. The program requires you to register phone numbers and email addresses you want associated with your account. Your best bet for making Textie useful is to convince others you know to also register their common information.

Textie allows both phone numbers and email addresses to be used as the recipient's destination. When someone wants to contact you, they enter either bit of data, and if it's registered with Textie, the message uses a few bytes of a 3G cellular plan or a Wi-Fi connection to move the information over. You can also include photos, which bumps up data usage slightly, but not much. Even with a 200 MB per month cellular data plan, heavy Textie usage will seem negligible.

With push notification enabled for Textie, incoming messages from the program pop up on screen just as with a carrier-backed text message. Textie does not have to be running. Messages are threaded by sender, too.

Textie can send outgoing cellular text messages at no cost to the sender to most U.S. networks due to a quirk in how these systems connect; T-Mobile and Sprint won't accept such messages at this writing. Recipients can reply.

Carriers charge 1,000 times more than their near-nothing costs. Textie turns that imbalance around. With little fuss, you can shave dollars off your phone bill by Textie-ing with your friends.

ACCOUNT: *Textie requires a free account to work.

Google Voice ▮▮▪

FREE* • Google • http://5str.us/2oy

Google Voice isn't an app yet, but it's just as useful

Google Voice isn't an iOS app—yet. It's a Web app that I include in this book for sheer utility, the only one of its kind here. Why? Because due to a seemingly long-running dispute between Apple and Google, an app version of Google Voice submitted in 2009 still hasn't been approved (nor has it been rejected) by Apple. U.S. government agencies are involved in the dispute.

But never mind that: why use Google Voice? Because it can let you work around the high price of international calling and domestic texting. The main Web app interface lets you place calls through an interesting workaround: you dial the number or select it from contacts you've defined. Google then sends you a text alert to dial one of its numbers. Tap Call and that number connects you to the other party.

For calls between two end points in the U.S., that doesn't make sense, as you're still using minutes from your voice pool. That's unlike Skype's or Line2's systems, which create pure data connections over 3G and Wi-Fi. But for international calls, Google Voice charges low per-minute rates while consuming U.S. minutes. (Calling a non-U.S. cell number outside of Canada and a few other countries, however, is still quite expensive on Google, Skype, or anyone.)

You can also send and receive text messages via Google Voice at no cost. And you can access incoming voicemail, which is roughly transcribed.

At some point, Google Voice will become a "real boy" and make it into the App Store, at which point it will compete directly with Skype, Line2, and other offerings. For now, the Web app is useful if you already use Google Voice to manage calls on your desktop.

Note: As the book went to press, Apple had approved two third-party Google Voice apps that act like souped-up Web apps, but were truly standalone programs. These apps don't provide VoIP calling or other call-around service. Nor are they written by Google. By the time you read this, a Google-built Google Voice app could be available.

ACCOUNT: *Requires free account. At this writing, accounts are only available in the United States, although Google Voice may be used worldwide by U.S. subscribers.

11

Travel & Navigation

Where do you want to go today? And how do you
plan to get there? Apps that can answer those
questions form the backbone of the utility of iOS.
Navigation and travel apps help you find your way
from point A to B to C by car (or see where you've
been en route), and help you travel through the air—
while coping with hassles on the ground.

INFORMATION / GPS NAVIGATION / TRACKING

TomTom U.S.A. ▪▪

$39.99 • TomTom International • http://5str.us/zjz

The power of a standalone GPS mostly transferred into iOS

TomTom is one of the giants in navigation hardware, and it's brought much of what made it a success there to its iOS app. Thoughtful changes were required to make it work on a smartphone.

Maps are included with the app, which boosts the size to over 1.3 GB. Each update to maps or program features requires a full download. But it's convenient to have the maps built in: no network connection is required en route.

If you want traffic updates—indispensible information for anyone who commutes by car, as far as I'm concerned—you buy for a separate $19.99-per-year in-app upgrade. Updates are sent every three minutes. (Traffic does require data access and use, but it's relatively minimal.)

TomTom offers a huge set of options for choosing a destination, including a

Google search, Contacts, entering an address, and finding nearby points of interest (POIs), like gas stations, hotels, or parks.

Navigation is presented quite well. By default, the map uses faux 3D (a flat 2D grid tipped to provide the feeling of distance). You can switch to 2D or see flat map representations of your map at any time. POIs are shown on the map, but you can choose which categories appear, including none at all. Spoken directions are generally clear, although the app really should know how to pronounce Los Angeles correctly (with a soft G, not the hard G of the Spanish original).

TomTom can work in the background under iOS 4 if you answer a call or switch to another app. With calls, navigation updates appear as on-screen push notifications. With another app, instructions are spoken while you're using that foreground program.

MORE: TomTom sells several versions of its app by country. Check the App Store for particular versions. Traffic update service is a $19.99-per-year in-app purchase, which requires a free account to set up.

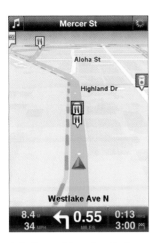

I pay a lot of consideration to how navigation apps interact with audio playback, as I'm often listening to music or a podcast in the car. TomTom lacks a built-in music player, found in some other programs. You can tap a musical note icon to pause and play music already selected in the iPod or other background audio app. Because of TomTom's iOS 4 support, however, you can just swap to an audio program to make changes without interrupting navigation.

The app also allows a separate adjustment to control whether spoken directions fade back music or audio, reducing its volume, or pause playback while speaking. You can even adjust the volume of spoken directions. In other apps that lack this control, the navigator voice may blare out substantially louder than a podcast or music—it's unnerving. The app can be set to speak numbers, streets, and traffic messages, or you can disable any or all.

The app also works with an external GPS kit for the original iPhone, iPhone 3G, 3GS, and, with an adapter, for the iPhone 4 ($99.95, **http://5str.us/mtz**).

A different kit is available for 2nd-generation and later iPod touch models ($79.95, **http://5str.us/ddf**). In testing, I didn't find much of an advantage for the iPhone kit, but iPod touch owners will like the option of using GPS navigation without requiring a phone plan.

Navigon MobileNavigator
$49.99 • Navigon • http://5str.us/lvb

Clearer maps and better audio control

This app is an excellent alternative to TomTom, with different strengths. Its key weakness? Navigon lacks robust address selection; you can't select from contacts, and address entry can be tedious.

But its navigation is top notch. The app presents streets and upcoming turns a bit better than TomTom, and shows retail and other POIs as a cleaner part of the landscape.

Navigon shines at audio support, with numerous options for controlling the interaction of spoken directions and music playback, including full iPod control within the app.

MORE: Navigon comes in many other editions, including ones specific to the U.S. west, central states, and east. Traffic update service is a $19.99-per-year in-app purchase.

MotionX GPS Drive

$0.99* • MotionX • http://5str.us/ht5

An inexpensive way to get from point A to B without a loss of quality

MotionX seems to have a mission to charge the least for turn-by-turn GPS navigation software of any product on the market. Fortunately, the firm doesn't forego quality in its drive for low cost.

It's also a useful collection of other location and navigation features beyond turn-by-turn directions, including compass, position, and nearby search.

You start at the menu, where you can tap Search and then one of several icons for a quick result. Icons correspond to airports, gas stations, food, and parking, and there are links for manual entry and a search for locations as well. Instead, you can tap Go To in the menu, and select from over 15 links there, including Zip code and Contacts.

The Position feature reveals your current precise coordinates, heading, and speed. But it also lets you tap one of three buttons to save the position, make it your home location (which is often a lot of fuss in other apps), or a "Park Spot." That last item adds your position to a parking spot list in the Go To menu.

The app doesn't include maps within itself, which makes it a tiny download at 11 MB. However, this means all data has to be pulled down over the air, and that can rack up cellular data bills if you travel extensively. Traffic information is included, but it's automatically figured into routes and not displayed as alerts.

The app does offer a simulation mode that can be run in advance of a trip to download and cache all the maps needed. The developers recommend running simulation at two times normal speed—it can run up to eight times faster—to have time to download all the necessary map pieces. You can set GPS Drive to hold up to 2 GB of cached map data, but you have to clear it out through an option in settings for fresher results.

MotionX is 99¢ for a 30-day trial of voice navigation. All other features remain active even if you don't subscribe. It has among the best voice navigation, with the clearest tone and best pronunciation. Voice navigation is linked to an account, which can be available to multiple devices, but only be active on one device at a time.

Audio playback support is terrific: a full iPod controller is available for selecting music and podcasts with options just like the iPod app; a mini-controller handles playback, shuffle, and repeat.

SUBSCRIPTION: *After 30 days, voice navigation costs $2.99 for a 30-day subscription or $24.99 for a year.
MORE: An iPad version is also available ($2.99, **http://5str.us/r5y**).

AT&T Navigator ▊▮

FREE* • AT&T • http://5str.us/6qo

Avoid traffic jams with this constantly updated subscription navigation aid

AT&T Navigator eschews features in favor of quality. Some competing navigation apps have the kitchen sink included, with dozens of preferences. But when you're setting up a route and driving, simplicity is key.

Choose a destination from your contacts, by address, or by searching for business names or types, and go. AT&T Navigator is the best app I've tried (out of 14 that I tested) at consistently finding Contacts addresses, where even Google Maps has failed.

A voice navigation option is fairly remarkable but not perfect. You can speak street numbers and addresses, and the app works hard to match, but can't always get it right. You can also

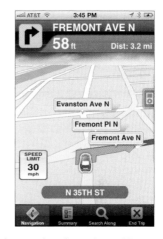

speak searches for points of interest, like a gas station or coffeeshop.

Traffic is part of the price of the monthly or yearly app subscription and is integrated within navigation. As you drive, you can tap Summary and select Traffic Summary to see what's ahead, or tap Minimize All Delays to reroute around jams. A Maps & Traffic view also allows you to see current traffic conditions wherever you want, and to tap on alerts for more details without a route plan.

Directions and other information are spoken by a pleasant voice that sometimes sounds a bit spliced together.

Maps and traffic updates download as they're required, and you need a cellular data or Wi-Fi connection to continue to view navigation if you vary from the planned route. This keeps the app compact and up to date, but can have an impact on your data bill.

SUBSCRIPTION: *Requires paid subscription: $9.99 per month or $69.99 per year.

Kayak ▉▪

FREE* • Kayak Software • http://5str.us/sn9

A shortcut to finding the best prices for flights, hotels, and more

Kayak keeps it simple despite the pile of different features under its hood. While the app focuses on price comparison for air fares, hotels, and car rentals, it also offers plenty of information: airport details (via GateGuru, next page), flight status, airline fees, bag fees, price alerts, currency conversion, and a whole lot more.

For starters, you turn to Kayak to save money. The free app gives you quick access to price results at many different travel sites. Those results are organized by a travel plan (like a particular set of flights) that you use to choose at which site to book. That includes Kayak's own booking service, if it's available for a given itinerary. You can also set alerts for a flight plan to be notified if the price changes. You can set those updates to appear daily or weekly—on screen and/or via email—and pick a price threshold above which you're notified.

The app's Buzz tab lets you see at a glance what the current prices are—best and average—for a route across a month. This can help if you are flexible about the dates you want to fly.

The app also books hotels and cars, letting you specify locations and landmarks. For hotels, I like the division into choice (a combination of value and

MORE: Kayak First Class removes ads and searches premium fares ($0.99, **http://5str.us/5ci**). A free iPad app is also available (**http://5str.us/v67**). **ACCOUNT:** *An optional free account syncs with Kayak.com.

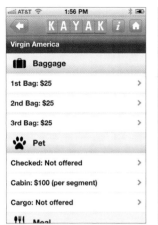

proximity), cheap, close, and classy; I may be classy, but my choice is cheap.

Kayak's app links to an optional free account at the Web site to sync up trips you've noted or planned on the site.

 GateGuru

FREE* • Mobility Apps •
http://5str.us/eji

Airport terminal information revealed and reviewed

Airline terminals seem designed to confuse, and perhaps they are. If we could see clearly how dreary it is waiting between flights maybe we'd fly less. GateGuru clears away the mist before our eyes, offering maps and amenity details for several dozen airports.

Airports are paired with information divided by terminals; if you don't know which terminal you're in (part of the airport's design, sometimes), tap Entire Airport, and then tap Map in the upper right corner.

If you pick a specific terminal, you see the amenities offered, as well as special offers from restaurants and clubs. Each terminal's detailed map is available, too. ATMs, restaurants, newsstands, bars, and other useful points of interest are paired with reviews left by GateGuru users. The reviews can be helpful in guiding you to a decent meal or an ATM without a huge surcharge.

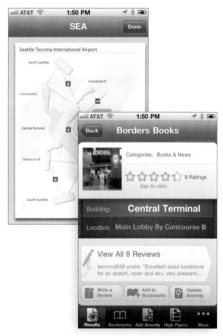

ACCOUNT: *An optional free account allows bookmarks and lets you leave reviews.

EasyTrails GPS

$4.99 • Zirak • http://5str.us/iin

If you don't know where you've been, how do you find it again?

If you hike, bike, stroll, or even drive paths regularly, you might want to stake out where you've been, and find out some information about the route, too. By foot or bike, tracking a trail lets you figure out distances and elevations for training or for tracking improvements.

EasyTrails GPS, which requires an iOS device with a GPS receiver, can record a track as you traverse it, and provide live and archived details. Even its main screen is useful after it gets a good GPS fix (indicated by the number of green bars): the page shows your current altitude, speed, and coordinates.

Tap the Rec (record) button, and the app starts tracking points along your route. You can tap pause or stop buttons along the way, or tap the trash can to cancel and delete the current route. Information about the track is displayed as you go, including the current altitude, speed, distance, and time elapsed, as well as the average speed underway, and the current coordinates. This is useful for exploring a path—and deciding if you might be going too far!

Three icons at the bottom provide alternate views: a compass shows the current heading; charts compare time, distance, and altitude; and the Map reveals the current route as recorded.

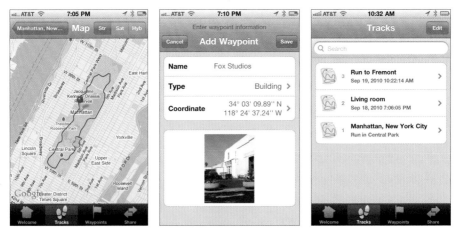

MORE: EasyTrails GPS Lite (free, **http://5str.us/39y**) tracks just one trail for 20 minutes but is otherwise identical.

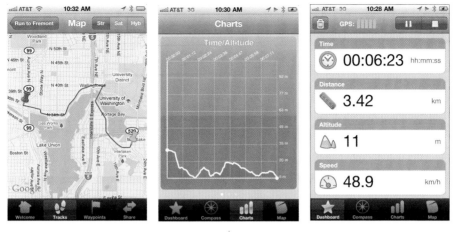

Map view has two other useful options. Tap the flag icon and you can add a waypoint, a set of coordinates to which you attach a name and can add a photograph. This can be helpful when planning a run or trip, and you want to associate a place with a mile marker. You can also tap the big R button and pull up a previous track to follow.

When your route is complete, tap the stop button in the Dashboard view, name and describe the track (both optional), and tap Save. The Tracks tab now shows your latest outing. You can review that route on a map, and examine charts.

As a long-time cyclist, I appreciate the altitude charts that are generated. I'm always wondering about the elevation of a given ride, wanting to see both how hard it was and compare it to other rides. Often, these elevation profiles are found only in guide books. EasyTrails shows both the altitude over time and over distance.

Runners will like the time over distance chart that lets them track their average speed at mile marks, as well as elevation charts for seeing hill performance.

Tracks can be exported to EveryTrail.com, emailed (in one of several common formats, including GPS, KML/KMZ, and comma-separated text), or accessed over a local Wi-Fi network using a Web browser. The last choice I haven't seen in other apps: you don't need WebDAV (p. xvi); just fire up a browser. The app runs its own Web server.

The app places configuration options in the iOS Settings app; that's where you choose units (feet/inches or meters), sound cues (when a GPS signal is lost or you're near a set waypoint), and security for Wi-Fi sharing.

FlightTrack Pro

$9.99 • Mobiata • http://5str.us/rrp

Frequent air travelers can rely on knowing which gate to run to and when

FlightTrack Pro aids the regular traveler—or the spouse, partner, or parent of one. The app tracks flights you enter, both upcoming and current. It can download flights listed in a free or paid account at TripIt.com as well. (The sync is one way; flights added in the app don't upload back to Tripit.com.)

Add flights in the app by tapping the plus sign on the home screen and selecting details. You can also shake the app and have a random current in-the-air flight added, useful for learning the app.

Active flights have a status screen that, when tapped, shows estimated and actual departure time, gate information, and stats about how likely the flight is to arrive on time. You can swipe down to add notes about the flight, call the airline, or find alternate flights.

Tap next to an airport's name and the app shows you the latest FAA delay information and weather reports.

An in-app upgrade in the iPad version reveals a flight board when you search for and select an airport (shown above).

Flights added in the app can be placed on your calendar, and the app automatically updates details as they change. You can forward information about the flight over email and SMS, or via Twitter and Facebook.

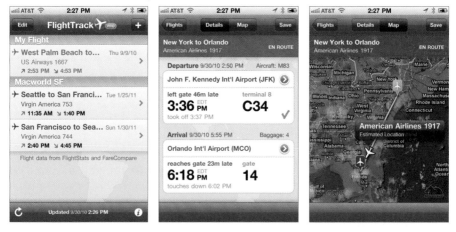

MORE: The non-pro FlightTrack omits TripIt sync, delay predictions, and push alerts for flights updates ($4.99, **http://5str.us/g9s**). FlightBoard offers just that display (universal, $3.99, **http://5str.us/kt1**).

12
Dining

Douglas Adam put it best in his *Hitchhiker's Guide to the Galaxy* series when he addressed the subject of food, describing the evolution of societies from needs to wants.

"The first phase is characterized by the question 'How can we eat?', the second by the question 'Why do we eat?', and the third by the question 'Where shall we have lunch?'"

RESTAURANTS / RECIPES

Yelp ▪▪

FREE • Yelp • http://5str.us/tcz

Reviews by other people of what's nearby, especially restaurants

Yelp brought peer review of restaurants, services, and other kinds of businesses to the Web. Previous efforts didn't seem to get large enough numbers to write up any but the best-known and largest firms and locations. The Yelp app brings its first-person insight to iOS, enhanced by location awareness.

Yelp's app is in many ways superior to the Web site, which has layers of navigation. The app shows what you need to know, stripped down for faster and easier searching, display, and reading. Tap the Nearby tab, and select the kind

of business you're looking for, and a list ordered by distance quickly appears.

Because Yelp has evolved into yet-another-social-networking site, you can also use the app to check-in at a location, notifying friends (and others, if you choose) that you're there, and achieve badges of honor for frequent check-ins. A Talk feature lets you have threaded discussions with those nearby.

Having a Yelp account and logging into the app gives you access to those features, but also lets you bookmark locations and retrieve business links you've noted. Yelp thrives on reviews, but you can only add "quick tips" via the app; reviews can be drafted in the app, but must be posted via Yelp.com.

The best and strangest option in Yelp is its Monocle mode, found in the Nearby tab's upper-right corner. Monocle puts labels on top of a live video display. This gives you a special Y-ray vision: reviews and other details float in virtual space as you move around. It's not perfect, but it's a combination of wayfinder and decision aid.

TIP: Tap the Sales & Special Offers category to see deals for Yelp users, as well as happy hours and other discounts.

OpenTable ▪▪

FREE* • OpenTable • http://5str.us/13j

Find a table near you and reserve it

Instead of calling around to a number of restaurants to see if you can get a table at the time you want, why not consult an app that can simply reveal what's available near you and when—and book the table, to boot. OpenTable's Web site has offered that service for years; the app provides a comparable experience.

OpenTable doesn't include all restaurants; only those that use its popular reservation system are part of the network. However, that includes many restaurants in major metropolitan areas. It's why you likely want Urbanspoon (p. 124), which links into the Rez system, installed on your device as well.

Most restaurants feature a menu (as an embedded Web page), reviews from registered OpenTable diners, and parking information.

The app combines discovery and searching. You can give it permission to use your location and then find restaurants near you with tables available that night. You can also enter a location and search by name. Reserving through OpenTable earns points redeemable at any restaurant that's part of the network.

OpenTable works best when you know what you want, but not how to get it.

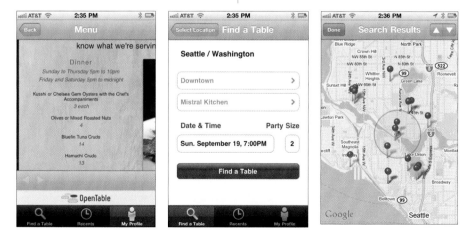

MORE: A separate free iPad version is also available (**http://5str.us/48j**). **ACCOUNT:** *An account is optional.

Urbanspoon

FREE • Urbanspoon • http://5str.us/443

Where to eat? Spin the wheel

With so many restaurants to choose from, perhaps spinning a wheel is the best choice when you don't know where to eat. Urbanspoon's wheel spinner spawned a lot of competitors, but its app started the trend.

Three wheels in the Shake tab show nearby neighborhoods, cuisine types, and price ranges. Shake your device around (but hold on tight) or tap the Shake button. The wheels spin, and where they land, there's your destination.

You can set a lock on one or more of the wheels to limit choices. Say you want cheap Vietnamese food or an expensive restaurant in the neighborhood you're currently standing in. I once used the app to find a hot dog restaurant to reward one of my children when I was in an unfamiliar neighborhood. (Schultzy's in the U District for the win!)

The Rez button, when locked, brings up only restaurants that have reservations available through the Rez system for that evening. (A competing system is used by OpenTable, p. 123; you may want both apps installed for that reason.)

Tap the resulting restaurant, or use any of the other tabs to find eating establishments, and the details for that location appear. Each restaurant's page shows a host of details, such as links (to a map, menu, and restaurant Web site), photos uploaded by patrons, a phone number, and a list of available reservation times for restaurants tied into Rez.

One of the consistently most useful items is the percentage, which shows the portion of all people who tapped the I Like It button rather than I Don't. The total votes are shown, too. This simple number corresponds quite well with the experiences I've had when visiting restaurants found through the app.

MORE: An iPad version is also available (free, **http://5str.us/ssy**).

Jai Thai (Fremont)
82% like it - 0.03mi - Thai - $

Beyond the percentage, there are also more detailed reviews from print media and online critics, as well as blog entries referring to the eatery and reviews left on Urbanspoon's Web site or via this app.

Friends also figure into this app. Tie in your Facebook account to share recommendations and see what your friends say about their dining decisions.

The Nearby map shows restaurants ordered by distance from where you're standing, although you can filter by cuisine and sort by name and ranking.

Tap the Scope button while holding your device more or less parallel to the ground, and a map appears centered on your current location with pins representing nearby restaurants.

Hold up your device, and iOS switches to video. After a moment, you see your surroundings overlaid by circles of varying diameters that are physically laid out in the direction of restaurants around you; the bigger the circle, the greater percentage of "I Like It" votes. You can pan your device to see more, or tap a circle to pull up additional information.

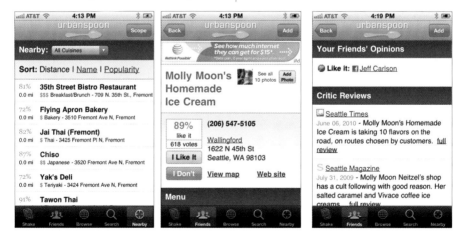

Dinner Spinner Pro

$2.99 • All Recipes • http://5str.us/6oa

Don't know what to make for dinner? Spin the wheel

It's far more difficult to figure out *what* to make for dinner or a potluck or a brunch than it is to make the food itself. Allrecipes.com offers its Dinner Spinner Pro as an aid. Tap the dial, the wheels spin, and suggestions arise. You can also choose by category (main dish, salads, and so forth), major ingredient, and time needed to prepare the meal.

The app taps into Allrecipes.com's vast archive of user-submitted and professional recipes, along with rankings and reviews. Rely on other users' feedback to figure out whether a recipe is worth making. We use Allrecipes.com all the time in my household; the wisdom of crowds works with cooking.

Recipes can be adjusted by the number of servings desired, and the appropriate ingredients dropped into a shopping list. You can view the nutritional information panel for any recipe, which adjusts based on servings.

Rotate your iOS device while viewing a recipe, and a special cooking view lets you more easily see the current step in a series of directions. Swipe down to access the full list of ingredients.

A free or paid Allrecipes.com account can be linked in to sync items in shopping lists and recipe boxes; no account is required, however.

This app goes well with iPhone or iPod touch stands—and perhaps a splashguard.

MORE: A free version available in several languages (**http://5str.us/rb6**) includes the spinner and searches, but excludes support for accounts, changing server sizes, and shopping lists.

13

Notes & Ideas

When inspiration strikes, strike back. Mobile devices should be able to capture the lightning in a bottle that emerges from our noggin. This chapter looks at apps that give you the tools to take roughly formed notions and preserve them.

Evernote

FREE* • Evernote • http://5str.us/k8m

Capture snippets, longer text, images, and more, with access from everywhere

Evernote is a way to capture whatever you're trying to keep track of without having to figure out how. When you use the firm's desktop software for Mac OS X or Windows, you can enter notes, snip sections of the screen, and grab Web pages.

But Evernote is equally useful in iOS; its software is also available for all other major U.S. smartphone platforms (no Nokia Symbian support, in other words).

The iOS app version lets you create text notes, annotate a photo, pull a picture from your camera roll, or make a voice memo.

Whenever you create any item in Evernote on your iOS device, it builds in the coordinates of your location (with

your permission). This allows notes to be placed on a map for finding later.

In fact, one tip that's provided with the app is to use Evernote as a way to remember where you parked your car. Snap a picture with your iPhone's camera, and then save that as a note. Later, when you've completely forgotten where you left your vehicle, use the

REQUIREMENTS: Evernote requires a free or paid account for sync. A free account offers 40 MB of uploads each month and limited file-type sync, and includes ads. Bump up to premium ($4.99/mo or $44.99 per year), and you

Notes view's search dialog. Tap in the search field, then tap Advanced Search beneath. Tap Near Here, and you can limit searches to within a mile. Voilà, your car!

The combination of note and location also means you can make geographically contextual notes when taking photos, traveling, or in lines of work in which you're out in the field observing.

The Evernote app synchronizes through the company's servers with all your other copies of the software on the desktop or on mobile devices. You can

also log into Evernote.com and use a well-designed Web app to gain access when away from all your hardware.

Flexibility and synchronization are key to turning Evernote into your outboard brain. You don't have to plan where you keep notes, snippets, and photos; they're always available wherever you go from whatever device you have.

Corkulous ▪️▫️

$3.99 • Appigo • http://5str.us/b6f

Stick a pin in it, virtually speaking

Corkulous simulates a large square cork board where you can pin photos, notes, to-do items, and tags. The idea is to provide the same kind of freeform organization a real cork board affords for brainstorming and moving items around, without the requirement to snip out and scrawl on pieces of paper. Best of all, you never run out of push pins.

The app provides a blessedly small number of choices: tap a file cabinet at the bottom of the screen, and you can add labels, sticky notes (which can be resized), to-do items that can be checked, contacts from your address book, and photos. In an Alice in Wonderland feel, you can also add tiny cork boards. Tap a cork board, and you're nested down a level into a fresh board. You can also create new boards at the top level of the app: either blank or from templates stored within it.

You tap an item to move it, and guides appear that help you line up edges with existing items on the board. Don't try to be too neat, however; this is just a simulation.

Double tap an item and you can edit its contents. For several kinds of notes you may change the typeface (from four informal faces) and increase type size via a slider. Double-tap a contact, and you can send him or her email, or switch to Safari to visit a Web site. (The full contact details are shown.)

Corkboards can be exported in multiple ways: via email; to the Photo Library; or using iTunes File Sharing (see p. xv) as a PDF file, image, or a special interchange format. Files in that format can be used with the app on other devices. When exporting to iTunes, you can choose to export the entire board, the current viewed area, or a selection you make by dragging a rectangle.

TIP: Use pinch and expand liberally to view a portion or an overview.

OmniGraffle ■■

$49.99 • Omni Group • http://5str.us/6fb

Create a visually connected presentation all with your fingers

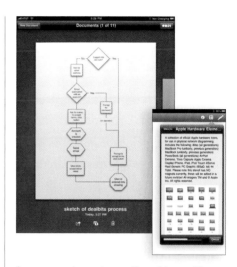

OmniGraffle for iPad is a way to create freeform and structured drawings that represent a flow of ideas. The program goes far beyond copying OmniGraffle for Mac OS X, although you can edit files in either program no matter which app created them.

The app instead is tailored for touch-based sketching and connection. You use OmniGraffle to create a flowchart, sketch out a sequence of ideas, or mock up what you want on a Web page. It's a blank sheet with formatting.

Create a new document, and tap the pencil icon at the upper right. The inter-face switches from green to brown, and tools appear for creating shapes or drawing.

Hold down on the square and you can draw a rectangle, ellipse, and other shapes. Tap the line-in-a-circle, and you can draw open lines, or enclose a space and it fills with color.

OmniGraffle is a star at connecting ideas, and the connection tool, when selected, lets you draw a smart arrow

from one shape to another. Move either shape and the connection persists; the arrow changes its direction as needed.

Switch back to the editing mode, and you can tap objects to resize them, insert text inside objects or on lines, and move connections. You can also add objects from a large library of stencils—prefab objects of all kinds. This library can be extended using desktop OmniGraffle stencils imported into the app.

Every element can be individually selected in a layers/objects menu. That menu also allows the creation and con-trol of layers.

Documents can be imported and exported through iTunes File Sharing. You can also email files in their native formats, or as PDFs or PNG images. Dropbox support would help this excel-lent app at managing files.

MORE: OmniGraffle for Mac OS X (**http://5str.us/ovn**) is available for $99.95.

MindNode ▇▪

$5.99 • Markus Müller • http://5str.us/caf

Organize your thoughts as a series of nodes of a tree, and turn them into to-do lists

Most of us can't claim to think perfectly in sequence. We have jumbles of ideas that we're trying to sort out. Mind mapping is one technique to take related ideas and link them together as "leaves of a tree." You start with a top node that represents a main concept, and "leaf out" with limbs of a tree extending out further and further as you develop ideas.

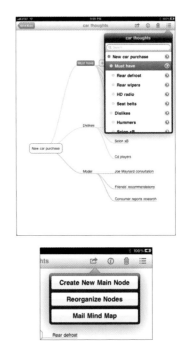

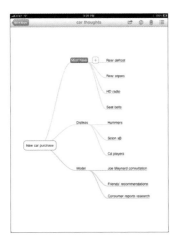

MindNode takes this concept to all iOS devices, letting you create maps with tap-and-type simplicity. Tap a main node and then tap a + to add a new subsidiary branch. Tap to select and then drag any node to move it (and its subsidiaries) to another part of the tree.

The graphical approach is good for sketching out ideas, but MindNode also lets you view the map as a text outline (tap the outline button at upper right).

As you work through creating a map, you can pinch and expand to see more or less at once. Tap a node and tap the trash can icon at top to delete its branch.

The app works with its desktop complement, MindNode (regular and pro versions) for Mac. You can transfer files to and from the desktop copy. A Wi-Fi transfer mode (a bit hidden under sync) shares over a local network using WebDAV (see p. xvi).

The app also allows mailing the node in several formats, including as text, an image, or an interchangeable file format used by many programs for outlines.

SimpleNote

FREE* • Simperium • http://5str.us/884

Take and sync notes wherever, archiving previous versions and sharing them

SimpleNote's nature is encoded in its name. The app and a complementary free Web site let you create notes. Notes sync between the app and the Web site (via a free or premium account) with no effort—I watched notes created on the Web site appear on in the app seconds later and vice-versa.

Notes can have tags assigned for filtering, and be pinned to keep them at the top of the list after you create newer items. Notes can be published with a link you share via the maker's Web site, shared with other SimpleNote users, or emailed.

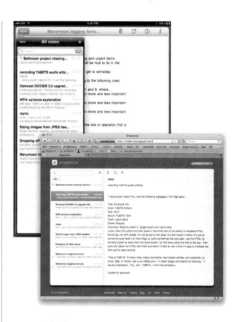

While composing or editing notes, you can tap the i button at the upper right to see the word and character count.

The service stores previous versions of notes (up to 10 for free accounts, 30 for premium). Tap the clock icon and you

can slide back and forth through version history. Tap Restore to bring back the older version.

The premium option, an in-app upgrade, adds an RSS feed, removes ads, and allows unlimited use of third-party programs that rely on SimpleNote storage.

UPGRADES: There are two In-app upgrades. Premium service is $11.99, and ad removal is $4.99.
ACCOUNT: *Requires free or paid account.

Outliner ▪▫▪

$4.99 • CarbonFin • http://5str.us/dtq

Structured way to create outlines and to-do lists

I was taught how to outline in the 6th grade, and recall being amazed: this is how someone could write a book, I exclaimed. (Warning: no outline was harmed in the creation of this book.) Outliner from CarbonFin is a solid effort to help you take a mishmash of ideas or tasks and put them into order.

The app lets you create as many items as you need, nested underneath one another in any fashion you like. It's a simple matter to tap a reorder icon (shown as two double-headed crossed arrows) and then drag it where you will. The program is clever enough to provide the right level of nesting as you move around among other items in your outline.

To promote or demote an item at one level, select the item, and then tap a promote or demote button (left and right arrows) to change how deeply in the hierarchy the entry is located.

Each item has a headline and an optional note, and that note can be quite long. It's the flexibility to write at length that lets Outliner transcend being just a list of bullet points.

Each item can be identified as a task or not. If a task, the entry has a checkbox. For elements that have entries hierarchically nested beneath them, a progress pie chart appears and shows how many tasks within have been completed.

A free, optional account allows syncing among multiple machines, as well as access from the Web site. (One missing piece: in the version tested at this writing, you can't reset the account on the app without reinstalling the software.) The Web site also lets you share outlines with other people through a published URL.

You can email your outlines (as text or in the OPML outline format) or access them from the Web site.

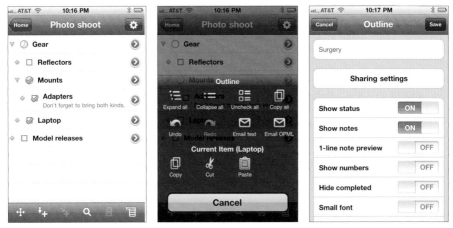

MORE: An iPad version of this app is also available ($4.99, **http://5str.us/cju**).

14

Information

Information, please.

With always-on Internet access, we should be able to find out the name of that uncredited actor in a 1956 movie wherever we want. And we can. But we can also find out the show time of the newest flicks (and book tickets), receive inspiration from remarkable people, scan barcodes on products and media, track our packages, and learn the differences between Iceland and Canada.

IMDB Movies & TV ■■

FREE • IMDB • http://5str.us/rtn

Can't remember that actress' name or every movie she appeared in?

The Internet Movie Database (IMDB) dates back to the early days of the widespread Internet; it just celebrated its 20th anniversary as I finished this book. Its goal then, as now, was to collect every fact about movies, ranging from cast and crew to obscure trivia. Television was later added into the mix. The app brings nearly the whole system to the mobile screen.

You can search on any term in IMDB from the app's main page, or use Movies, TV, and People buttons to follow links like top-grossing movies, the nightly television broadcast schedule by show, or actors with a birthday on the day you're checking. You can even get a summary—*spoilers!*—about shows you missed the previous few days.

Movie and TV show detail pages are a summary of the full site's information, showing cast and crew, and votes and reviews (both critics and user-submitted). An actor's page shows the movies and TV shows he or she is best known for, with a tap to see the full filmography.

Each production and person page also has a link at the bottom to open the full IMDB.com Web page within the app.

If you let the app know your location, you can view movie showtimes at theaters near you, too.

TIP: Links to buy film and TV shows on DVD are throughout the app. IMDB was bought years ago by Amazon.com, but the only way this shows is through these convenient links.

Bing

FREE • Microsoft • http://5str.us/et3

Attractive, efficient Web and image search that makes good use of iOS

Bing is Microsoft's answer to Google Search, and it's a pretty good one. Bing's results on the Web are often more germane, better filtered, and better organized. While you can use the Settings > Safari > Search Engine option to switch your Mobile Safari browser from Google to either Bing or Yahoo! for searching, the Bing app has a lot to offer as a standalone look into search results.

Enter a search term into the main field in the app, and results for maps, Web pages, images, and news appear. Links from all four categories (plus suggestions for other searches at the bottom) can be viewed in the app.

The image view is particularly good. It shows a screen of thumbnails matching the result. As you swipe downward, new thumbnails are loaded row by row endlessly (or until there are no more matches). Tap for a preview, and tap Full Screen for a higher-resolution preview.

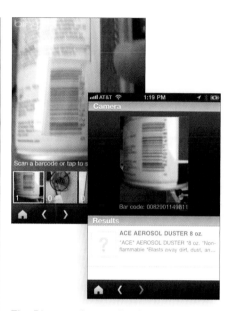

The Bing app has evolved, however, from a simple search replacement to an attempt at encapsulating everything you might want to do on the Web or in another app. You can find travel deals, movie times, connect to Facebook and Twitter, shop, and get the news and weather. It's ambitious, but well-presented, and you can simply ignore the parts you don't need.

However, don't miss the Camera mode on the app's home page (swipe left on the list of links at the bottom to find the Camera label). Tap Camera, and Bing automatically scans media or other bar codes to bring up matching items; or tap when a book or album cover is centered, and have Bing find an item match and link to search results for it.

Delivery Status

$4.99 • Junecloud • http://5str.us/lda

Track packages' delivery status

The Internet was supposed to cut down on the amount of physical stuff we dealt with. Yeah, right. Like many people, I have packages in transit all the time from Amazon and other e-tailers, returns heading back, and repairs somewhere in between.

Keeping track of such items requires visiting many different Web sites. Delivery Status puts your purchases and shipments all in one location. The app connects to a few dozen postal services, delivery companies, and online shops (Adobe, Amazon, Apple, and Google Checkout) to pull down the latest location of a package or envelope.

With online stores, you can plug in your username and password along with the appropriate order number, and the app pulls in details for you. For shippers, you enter a tracking number, and the program consults the delivery firm's Web site directly.

The current location of an item can be shown on a map, although that's a little bit of eye candy: if I have an Apple product that's in Shengzhen, China, it doesn't help me much to see it on a map. Tap View Details Online and an inset Web window of a package's progress is pulled from the postal or other service.

Delivery Status works with an optional free account for synchronizing your package information across devices and the Web site. There's a free Mac OS X widget that can also tie into this synced delivery data.

Parcel

FREE • Ivan Pavlov • http://5str.us/ivd

A well-designed free package tracker

Simply designed, Parcel works with fewer shipping companies and postal services than Delivery Status, but has all the main ones.

Parcel shows the full transaction history as a package changes hands from shipper to your door without requiring an extra tap. The app shows a few shippers by default; use the Settings app to add others or remove those displayed.

UPGRADE: Parcel has a $1.99 in-app purchase that adds push notifications and the ability to track more than 3 shipments at once.

Movies by Flixster ■■

FREE* • Flixster • http://5str.us/geb

A one-stop movie hub for finding films, reading reviews, and buying tickets

Flixster is a one-stop film machine, offering reviews, ticket buying, actor information, trailers, show times, and much more. The associated site is a sister to the user-driven movie review site Rotten Tomatoes, and its ratings—percentages alongside a squished fruit for a pan or a plump one for a rave—are shown along with access to reviews. Critics rankings and reviews are included, too.

Each movie has—where available—trailers, photos, showtimes, and reviews, and links for cast members. You can tap Add My Rating (if logged in) to provide your opinion.

My favorite use of Flixster is to find where I can see a current film; it's also great for finding a movie—and use its ratings to see whether there's one worth seeing.

Set your location from the My Movies tab (scroll down to tap Settings, then tap

Location). Now from any movie listing in the Box Office tab, you can drill down to see at which theaters it's playing. A map link can help decide which one. If there's a theater you like, the Theaters tab tells you what's playing on its screens.

Some theater listings offer a Buy link for purchasing tickets directly within the Flixster app.

WolframAlpha ▪▫

$1.99 • Wolfram Alpha • http://5str.us/usq

Informational queries at your fingertips, no matter how obscure

If you ask WolframAlpha, "What's the meaning of life," it tells you the correct answer: 42. The company must have a fan of *The Hitchhiker's Guide to the Galaxy*. More seriously, however, you can throw a remarkable variety of questions at the system, and get structured responses.

WolframAlpha processes questions or fragments you ask, and tries to find data sources that match, including comparisons. If you type in "Seattle vs. Bellingham," the system provides square miles, population, unemployment, and the distance between two points. Enter "gold vs. silver," and the periodic table appears plus much more.

For math, the app shines, which is no surprise given that Wolfram is the leading creator of graphical mathematical equation software. You can punch in any equation, and have the solution neatly presented.

This includes such minor esoterica as asking for X digits of π or e, but also deep differential equations.

While WolframAlpha is free to use at the Web site, the format isn't quite as compact as the app, which allows you to read results in an easy-to-scan fashion; forward answers via email, Twitter, and other methods; and run through tutorials for using the system.

WolframAlpha doesn't contain all the information in the universe, but what it has it exposes better than Google.

TED Mobile

FREE • Willflow • http://5str.us/1uv

Geniuses available on tap to inform and inspire

The TED conference is where geniuses, rich people, celebrities, and academics go to listen to people even smarter or more interesting than themselves. But the main conference has a steep price tag—$6,000!—and the organizers have spawned separate events, as well as authorizing offshoots on topics like the Gulf oil spill. Too much to handle?

You don't have to come with that kind of scratch or travel the globe to get TED's insight, due to a bit of generosity from the conference organizers. The videos from these events are now freely available via the Web. Because Web video is awkward and sometimes impossible to view on a mobile device, the TED Mobile app packages all that video in a way that's easy to search, browse, and view.

Talks are organized by theme and tags. Themes focus on big picture concepts like The Rise of Collaboration and Not Business as Usual. Themes

also highlight regional TED events like TEDIndia. Tags broadly divide content into a bit over a dozen categories, such as humor and business.

The Ted Talks icon takes you to the most recent talks in order of posting. You can also tap Search to find presentations by name or description.

Tap any talk for more details. You can also mark a talk with a star to find it under Favorites later. You tap to watch talks just like any embedded movie. TED Mobile is inspiration in your pocket.

TIP: After tapping a tag or theme, tap the icon at the bottom to return to the main list.

QuickMark 4 ■■

$0.99 • SimpleAct • http://5str.us/ye7

Snap bar codes and 2D tags and turn them into URLs or text

Have you seen those squares full of dots that look like they're supposed to mean something? And have you seen more of them lately? Those are 2D (two-dimensional) bar codes or tags, and are increasingly attached to restaurant doors, products, and kiosks. They've even started to show up in ads on cable television!

QuickMark 4 can read these codes and convert their information into text, which is often a URL. You can jump to the URL or store it for later. The app can also decipher codes that contain plain text, a phone number, or other information.

The app supports the two most popular kinds of 2D tags: QR Codes and Data Matrix. The program can also scan and read most 1D barcodes, including those used on books and on retail products.

The app can share information, too, using Bluetooth to send decoded tags to another device running the same app, or via Wi-Fi to a Mac on the same network using a simple piece of free software provided by the developers.

QuickMark 4 can also generate QR Codes from information you provide, including one of your contact, a URL, or other information that you enter. In a bit of the snake eating its own tail, you can create a code from a code you just scanned for sharing.

REQUIREMENTS: This app requires an iPhone 3GS or 4 or a 4th-generation iPod touch. An earlier version of QuickMark (**http://5str.us/v8l**) is still available for sale for older phones running iOS 3.

RedLaser ■■

FREE • eBay • http://5str.us/vtt

Find products by bar code with a scan

A bar code is a portal into a wealth of information, but it's often tedious to get from the pattern or numbers associated with it to results. RedLaser automates that process with a single tap required to get started.

Find any consumer item with a barcode, whether it be a book, a can of chowder, or a piece of software. Tap the lightning bolt icon and hold the camera lens over the barcode. Onscreen alignment bars help you orient the code; the bars light up green when they are over the right place. The app works even with the 1st-generation iPhone.

After it extracts the numbers, RedLaser searches Google and other sites for results. The results are divided by site, and include links for purchase. eBay bought this app from its original developers, and naturally eBay and Half.com links appear—though neither at the top nor with any special treatment.

For books, the app matches (using location with your permission) holdings in nearby libraries. You can even tap through to the library page for the item.

TIP: Use RedLaser to scan the barcode of books or movies at friends' houses, bookstores, or libraries to keep a running book list and to compare prices at online stores for purchase.

Animated Knots

$4.99 • Grog • http://5str.us/6zy

A pocket guide to every knot you need to tie

You can't underestimate the importance of knots, which used to be taught to every child in scouting, on a farm, and at school. Knots now seem old fashioned despite their everyday utility in the home for building projects, in sports, and in emergencies.

Animated Knots is a terrific way for those with little knot-tying experience to have a pocket guide to many dozens of common knots, organized by category. (Some knots appear twice when they're useful in more than one place.)

Better yet, Animated Knots animates the knot tying—seems kind of obvious by its name, no? The app offers written instructions, and then step-by-step photos that you can watch. As each step completes, the corresponding text in the description is highlighted.

Tap the i button and you can drill deeper into alternatives for the knots. You can follow links from the additional information, view knots by name, and add knots to a favorite list.

 ## Knot Guide

$1.99 • Winkpass Creations • http://5str.us/yma

A knot compendium without the animation, but with great directions

For a little less money, you can opt for Knot Guide. The app omits playable animations, but has nearly 100 knots with steps illustrated by photos with captions that you tap to page through. It's a little less convenient than Animated Knots, because you have to tap through, but it provides larger photos, and may appeal to people who want to flip back and forth more readily.

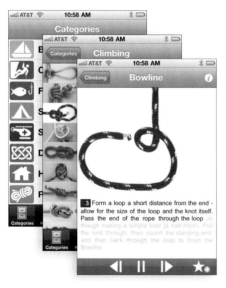

15

News & Sports

The 24-hour news cycle can be tapped to your advantage using apps that filter the flood of information into nuggets you can consume. These apps help you make sense of the world—and keep track of the latest baseball scores.

NYTimes

FREE • The New York Times • http://5str.us/gkp

All the news fits; no print

If you like to read the best newspaper in the world, there's no better place than the NYTimes app. The company hasn't made its Web site well suited for mobile browsing, but the app provides ready access to top stories and makes it easy to drill down for more.

The approach is simple: four section tabs along the bottom and a More button to reach the rest of the virtual paper.

Tap a tab like Latest, and the news fills the screen as a series of horizontal items with blurbs. Tabs reload with any newer items; you can tap the reload button in the upper right to force this behavior if you think the section is out of date.

Tap a story, and you're in an article view, which often has a photo at the top. Tap in the middle of the page to hide the top and bottom navigation, which increase the readable area and remove interface distraction of buttons. The app works equally well in portrait and landscape orientations for reading and navigation.

The left/right arrows at the upper right on a story page let you move among stories in the section, while an action button at lower left passes on the story via email, text messaging, or Twitter; you can also copy the link from the action menu. Tap Save, and the article is stored on your device.

The Times would be wise to link in directly with Evernote, Instapaper, and others to save links and snippets for later reading across the Web and your various devices. I don't mind having ads inserted, but I'd rather have more ways to remember what I wanted to read.

Your position within a story isn't captured; if you exit and return, you have to navigate back to where you left off. The app would be far better if the last-read location were noted, as in the Kindle, iBooks, and Nook apps for ebooks.

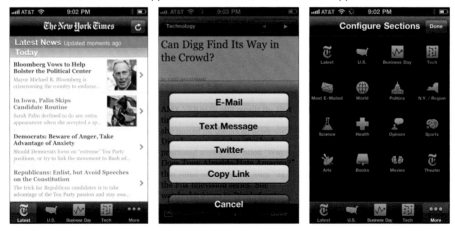

TIP: While the app is open, even while asleep, it continues to pull down stories and photos. You can turn this off in the Settings app; swipe down to NYTimes and change the Synchronization options for EDGE & 3G and Wi-Fi.

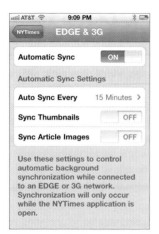

If you don't like the four default sections placed at the bottom of the home screen, tap More, and then browse through all the other departments at the paper. Tap Edit and you can drag new sections to the bottom to replace the ones that are there.

More also hides the Search and Saved Articles links: swipe to the very bottom to find them. Via Search, you can find any article at the paper in the last few days. When I configure the app, I tend to move Search to the main page.

Enjoy this app's no-cost availability while you can, as the New York Times plans to add subscription fees in some fashion to mobile access and its Web site in 2011.

NYT Editor's Choice
FREE • The NewYork Times •
http://5str.us/c4u

Leading stories in a print layout

The free iPad-targeted version includes a much more limited selection of stories laid out in a more pleasing newspaper-like format. Searching isn't allowed. It sometimes seems like more of an experiment than real intent, but it's a delight to read in this format. I highly suspect that when the Times starts charging for news, you'll see the iPhone/iPod touch app and this one merge into one with far better flexibility.

For now, one of the highlights of the iPad app is watching recent videos from the Times extensive documentary operation. This includes shorts by the popular David Pogue, a colleague and the Times' tech columnist, as well as video footage from all over the world.

The other bright point is reading in long form. Feature articles of many thousands of words are easy to read on the iPad over several screens; not so with the NYTimes app on its littler brethren.

Bloomberg ▪▪

FREE • Bloomberg • http://5str.us/eg8

Single-stop shop for financial news and analysis

Bloomberg is the recognized world leader in financial news, and its free app distills a massive body of up-to-date reports and data into an easy-to-browse format. You can pull up stock charts, add stocks and indices to a custom port-folio, and read general financial news as well as reports related to specific market items.

The app also includes bond, commod-ity, and currency values, and a variety of indices and index futures.

Regularly updated podcasts (some daily) can be found as well. The iPad version (see figure at upper right) presents the same data with more of a dashboard feel, revealing more information in an at-a-glance format.

Those who work in the financial indus-try and have Bloomberg terminals can tap into the MSG system, and send and receive messages.

MORE: An iPad version is also available (free, **http://5str.us/kzn**).

NPR

FREE • NPR • http://5str.us/1wr

Public radio junkies will find the broadcasts, playlists, and transcripts invaluable

Beware the siren call of the NPR app: it provides an endless stream of the programs public radio listeners want. After you start using it, you may leave it running constantly. (I'm addicted to *Wait Wait Don't Tell Me* and *Planet Money*.)

You might think that with downloadable podcasts, an app focused on streaming audio wouldn't be that useful. But NPR has packed in the kind of organization, access, and detail that makes it indispensible for those who love public radio.

A News tab provides access to the latest reports, which you can read as text or listen to. A Newscast view within News offers the latest hourly summaries, too.

The app also lets you efficiently manage your listening. In the Programs tab, the app shows all network programs. (Many folks are surprised to find that National Public Radio is but one of several public-radio networks. The others so far lack good apps.)

Tap a program, and you can add segments or everything currently available for that program to your playlist. For archived programs, there's a Get Podcast link that launches the iTunes app and switches to the entry for that program to download episodes.

If the On Air label is next to the program name, you can opt to stream the program live from a member station. The app provides a list of those currently broadcasting the program in real time.

In the Playlist tab, all the segments you've added are shown. Tap to listen, and the segment starts streaming. The tab also lets you delete entries.

The app helps you find stations by Zip code or your proximity so you can pick a station to stream live.

If you want to share a link to a segment, the app allows Facebook posting, tweeting, and sending email.

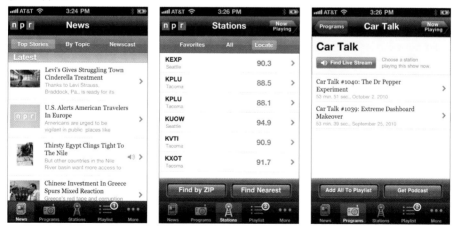

MORE: NPR also has an iPad app that presents the same results in a slightly easier-to-use format (free, http://5str.us/1nh). NPR offers a music app as well (free, **http://5str.us/gyl**).

At Bat 2010 for iPad ▮▮▪

$14.99 • MLB Advanced Media • http://5str.us/2z6

It's almost like being at the ballpark

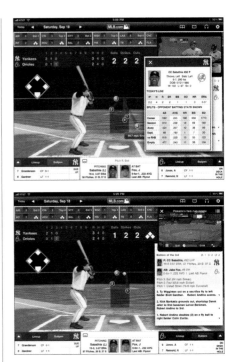

The Internet brought a multitude of ways for fans to enjoy more access to games outside their home broadcast market. Mobile devices take that further, providing live and archived audio, video, and gameplay diagrams wherever you are.

At Bat 2010 for iPad is the current apotheosis of such apps: it's Major League Baseball in your satchel, formatted for the iPad's page. The app is focused on live games with deep archives after they're played.

You have a few options on how to start. Tap the book pages icon in the upper right and choose Gameday, and you're thrown right into the action.

A leaderboard at the top shows the current day's games along with scores for games that are underway or complete. Tap on a game, and it expands to fill the screen. For games still being played, the app shows a graphic of the field from the batter's point of view, including whether he's a left, right, or switch hitter.

At the top of the live view, the app displays a scoreboard with current balls,

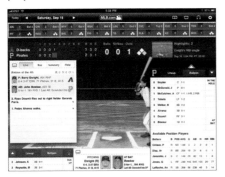

strikes, and outs. In the main view, you see a depiction of who is on base. As pitches are thrown, the app shows the rough passage of the ball from pitcher to strike zone, labeled by the order of pitches, and with the speed of the ball. (You can tap the order number to bring the speed back up.)

Along the bottom, you can access the lineup and bullpen for the visitors and the home team. Tap an arrow, and the whole list pops up. Tap a player to get his card and stats.

The middle box at bottom has live details about who's pitching and at bat. Tap its

MORE: iPhone/iPod touch versions are available for $14.99 (http://5str.us/wko) and free (http://5str.us/4ka); the free version omits day of game audio, pitch-by-pitch, and box scores.

popout button, and a window overlays the screen with four tabs to keep track of the game, showing live text narrative about the action so far. The popout also reveals a detailed box score, an inning-by-inning summary, and a top view of a field schematic. But, wait, there's more! The field map shows who's at which position ("What's on second?"), the distance for crossing fences in the outfield, and the on deck and in-hole players.

The text presentation is detailed and well written, but you don't have to just read. Tap the headphones icon at the top right, and you can select the live commentary. The tabs let you choose between either the home town or away announcers. If you have a subscription to a $99 or higher MLB.tv package, you can view live video for games that aren't blacked out in your area.

During the game, everyone can view instant highlights; after the game there's no subscription required to view a condensed version of the action. This summary video is up to 30 minutes long and becomes available fairly quickly following a game's completion.

That Gameday display is just the tip of the information iceberg. Tap that book icon again, and you can select Scoreboard or Standings.

Scoreboard shows the box scores for every game played on a given day, with access to past days' scores. Tap a box score and you get a window into the details, video, and other stats.

The Standings screen shows the current order of teams in each league, as well as post-season wild-card standings.

NOTE: The At Bat app will be updated each year, requiring a new purchase for the current season according to plans at this writing. The 2010 app's price went down in late-season play as it neared the end of its lifespan.

16

Writing & Painting

Creativity comes bursting out of us at inconvenient moments. That's why it's useful to have a mobile device capable of letting us express ourselves with no intermediation. We can draw on the glass or tap our words directly in. The apps in this chapter provide a direct conduit for our outpourings.

PAINTING / LAYOUT / WRITING

Brushes ▮▮▯

$7.99 • Steve Sprang • http://5str.us/yzv

Makes a mobile device a true "multimedia" canvas

Brushes is a hit with artists, who rely on the software to create rich, layered paintings along with photographic manipulations and overlays. You choose from a small array of brushes, which are actually a repeated object that you can add spacing between, to produce a solid line, speckles, and other effects.

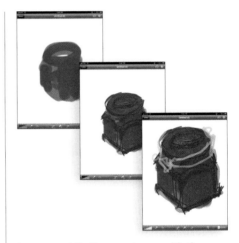

Transparency controls for color provide a fine adjustment. Overdrawing adds additional opacity as with watercolors. A brush option lets you choose to let speed affect the brush width and opacity. Draw more slowly and a thicker, less transparent "paint" layer is applied.

Onscreen controls for bringing up editing tools are well thought out: a double tap in one corner performs an undo; a double tap in another lets you change the weight of the brush or eraser.

The layers control is superb, allowing the ability to create, shuffle, and preview layers and flatten one layer with the next via a tap. Photoshop-like combination effects, like darken and multipy, are available. Varying opacity and effects can produce remarkable paintings.

If you want to start with a photo, you can tap the photos icon in the upper right and select a picture from your Photo Library. The image can be scaled and rotated before being placed on the page.

Brushes even sneaks in an extra feature beyond just exporting to the photo library or sending via email: you can turn the app briefly into a network file server to retrieve files directly from a Mac or Windows computer using WebDAV (see p. xvi).

MORE: Brushes also comes in an iPhone/iPod touch version ($4.99, **http://5str.us/dkl**).

SketchBook Pro ■■

$7.99 • AutoDesk • http://5str.us/vj6

The makers of the leading CAD software have an artistic side, too

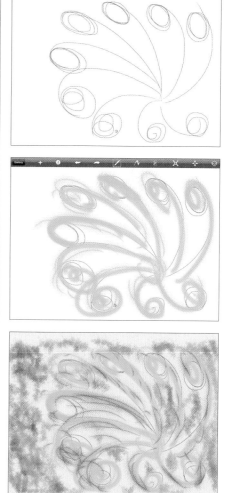

AutoDesk was an unlikely company to offer a painting and drawing program, but it was among the first to do so for the iPad. The firm is best known for CAD/CAM software used by architects, industrial engineers, and manufacturers. But SketchBook Pro doesn't suffer from an engineering mindset.

Brushes (previous page) makes virtual drawing feel more like the real thing, but offers fewer brush types and options for variations. If you like to work among many different kinds of simulated media, SketchBook Pro has a leg up.

The app has an array of 75 brushes, pens, sprays, and odd stamps like hands and vertebrae. A brush preview shows you a stripe of the brush as you adjust color, radius, and opacity.

SketchBook Pro provides solid layer control with an opacity slider for creating overlaid drawings. You can set how each layer combines with the ones below, and reorder layers by dragging.

SketchBook Pro can export drawings as Photoshop files with layers intact or you can flatten a drawing. Your work can be added to the iPad Photo Library, emailed, or copied via iTunes. The app can also import photos into layers.

MORE: An iPhone/iPod touch version is also available as SketchBook Mobile ($2.99, **http://5str.us/yzr**). There's also a free version with some limitations, named SketchBook Mobile Express (**http://5str.us/p2m**).

Pages ▇▮

$9.99 • Apple • http://5str.us/ggt

Sophisticated page layout on the iPad interchangeable with a Mac

Pages is Apple's flagship on the iPad to prove it's a device as well suited to creating as consuming. Other apps throughout this book make that point as well. Pages for iPad is designed to work as interchangeably as possible with the Mac OS X Pages app, part of iWork.

formatting bar/rule combination at the top includes styles for headings and other categories of text. You can also select text and add formatting such as bold and italic, and set left, right, fully justified, and centered alignment.

For the most part, it succeeds after an awkward start. The version of Pages reviewed for this book was robust enough to allow two-way file transfers and create serious documents.

Pages creates both documents and page layouts while blurring the line between them. You start with a template that already has elements in place for a given task, like composing a letter on letterhead or creating a flyer. The Blank template is available, too, for starting out fresh.

Let's start with text. You can tap in a document and just start typing. A

More formatting options are hidden behind the i button at top. Tap that button, and the app reveals style and type formatting options, but also the List and Layout tabs. Select text and use the List tab to set bullet or numbered/lettered formats. The Layout tab offers aligment

---

MORE: Pages for Mac OS X is part of iWork ($79, **http://5str.us/jbv**). Apple offers a free downloadable trial.

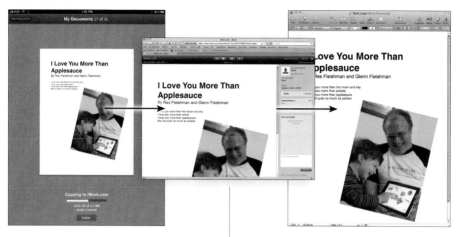

controls, but also can also set selected text to span multiple columns, and increase or decrease line spacing.

On the graphics side, tap the picture icon to grab photos from your Photo Library, or insert tables, charts, and shapes. Imported pictures can be rotated with a two-finger gesture, cropped, and resized.

Apple borrowed a page, pun intended, from its Numbers app for handling charts and tables. Tap a table, and it's inserted. Cells and headers can be edited and formatted via the i menu.

Grab a chart and then double-tap it on the page to access its underlying spreadsheet. You can enter data there, while the i menu controls X and Y axis formatting, among other details. Change the data, and the chart changes.

The combination of built-in options should let you create nearly any document or at least a complete first pass at it. For more detailed text, graphics or output control, you can swap the document into the desktop version of Pages.

Tap My Documents at the upper left and select a document. Tap the forward icon and several options appear. You can email, copy for iTunes File Sharing access, transfer to a WebDAV server, or upload to your MobileMe iDisk. For each option, you can choose to export as a native Pages file, a PDF, or a compatible Word document.

You can also export to iWork.com, which requires a free account. iWork lets you share documents with other people (see the workflow at the top of the page), but it's still clearly a work in progress.

Pages also imports files from iTunes File Sharing, iDisk, or a WebDAV server.

Elements

$4.99* • Second Gear • http://5str.us/v6m

Edit text files directly from Dropbox

This app tries to be just about the simplest word processor you could use on an iOS device. It's all about the writing.

Files are stored on the hardware only temporarily; Dropbox, an Internet-hosted file service, acts as the hard drive (see p. 171 for more on Dropbox).

You can choose among iOS fonts and set the type size, font color, and background, and that's nearly all you have access to or need. Elements supports TextExpander macros (p. 186) for quicker entry as well.

Documents are saved when you tap Done; you can also email a copy of the document. Files are saved into an Elements folder in your Dropbox storage. You can copy and add files to that folder directly.

Plain Text

FREE† • Hog Bay Software • http://5str.us/jjd

In the same vein, but simpler

Plain Text has even fewer settings than Elements. It also taps into Dropbox, and works with TextExpander macros. However, Plain Text can work with any Dropbox folder chosen when you enter your Dropbox account details. Dropbox isn't required, as the app also allows files to be copied in and out via iTunes Sharing using USB (see p. xv).

Plain Text lets you set when changes are synced with Dropbox. The default is practically when anything happens: when the app is launched or exited, when you make an edit, and when you open a file or folder.

The austere nature of the app should lend itself to undistracted composition.

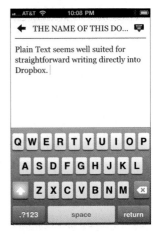

TIP: Both apps support the standard undo: shake the device to get a prompt to reverse the last changes.
ACCOUNT: *Requires free or paid Dropbox account. †Makes use of an optional free or paid Dropbox account.

17

Nature

With our head down using a mobile device, we might miss the rest of creation. The apps in this chapter make us lift our eyes to look in wonder—and with knowledge—at the sky above and the world around. Or at least see if it's raining outside.

The Elements ▮▮▮

$13.99 • Theodore Gray • http://5str.us/4p9

There's antimony, arsenic, aluminum, selenium...and over a hundred more

Science geeks love the periodic table of the elements. Some even carry around a wallet-sized card in case there's a sudden need to know the atomic weight of molybdenum (it's 42).

What better way to demonstrate the range, depth, and capriciousness of the universe in which we live? The periodic table divides indivisible building blocks of existence (let's ignore quarks and gluons for a moment) by how many electrons are required to fill a shell, and orders them by the number of protons in the nucleus (from least to greatest).

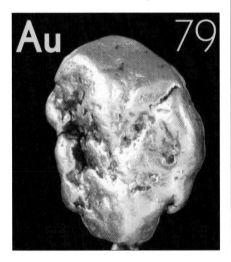

Theodore Gray, one of math software developer Wolfram Research's founders, has spent an enormous amount of time, money, and effort collecting examples of every element that's extant, and documenting them. (Some elements are created under high-energy conditions and

have miniscule lifetimes before breaking down. These are obviously a bit hard to picture.)

He's produced books, a Web site, and now a glorious app, one of the first available for the iPad when it was released. The app shows the periodic table with photography, information, and links to Wolfram Alpha (see p. 140) for additional data lookups.

As a teaching and learning tool, The Elements is marvelous, bringing dry mechanical facts into sharp color and live interaction.

For each element, you can see a large sample—as found in nature or manufactured into a product—of an item containing the element. That example can be swiped and tapped to spin and rotate in three dimensions around a single axis.

The main page reveals a host of information at a glance: the position of the element on a schematic color-coded periodic table at top; the atomic radius and organization of electrons in shells;

MORE: A version for the iPhone 4 and 4th-generation iPod touch is also available ($9.99, **http://5str.us/yih**).

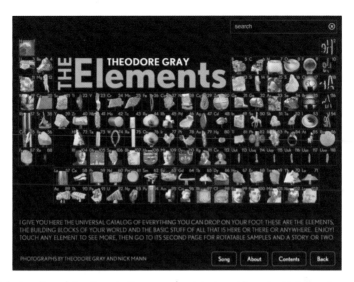

the crystal structure (also in rotating 3D), with a description; and a number of statistics to define the element in relationship to the rest of the universe.

A set of colored lines across the right side from top to bottom represent the atomic emissions spectrum—the wavelengths emitted when an element is superheated.

On the detail page for the element, there are typically several other examples throughout well-written text; each of those images may also be rotated. Double-tap any image, and you get a

side-by-side set which can be used with stereographic glasses. (Mr. Gray offers an inexpensive pair through his site for about $8 with shipping within the U.S.)

The app has stolen my heart because it opens with a song: 1950s–60s comic singer (and Harvard mathematician) Tom Lehrer's "The Elements," a rendition of all elements known in 1959, sung to the tune of a Gilbert and Sullivan song. The song is animated with each element appearing as Mr. Lehrer sings it.

For young scientists and those young at heart, hours can be whiled away examining the little things that make us up.

NOTE: Wolfram is another name for the element tungsten.

Star Walk ■■

$4.99 • Vito Technology • http://5str.us/v7v

Take a magic window into the stars with you while you gaze

When sitting outside on a crisp, clear night, did you ever wish constellations and stars had labels? Star Walk fills that desire for folks like me who know a smattering of stars, but can only reliably find a few.

The app uses GPS and other positioning sensors to provide something like "augmented reality," where the world around you is annotated with details. (Automatic positioning requires a compass sensor, which is built into all iPads.)

Hold an iPad up to the sky outside, and it's like you have a true magic window. Constellations fade in automatically when you pause over a view. Tap any star, galaxy, or other feature, and you can then tap an information button to see a close-up with more detail.

Star Walk also has a remarkable fast-forward/rewind mode for moving through time as well as space. Tap part of the date, like the year, spin the dial by

flicking up or down, and watch the stars move as if you were in an Einsteinian inertial frame of reference traveling at a fraction below the speed of light. You can also move in small increments.

A "local neighborhood" view shows you various details about the current phases of the moon, when planets appear in the sky, and sunrise and sunset.

MORE: Star Walk also comes in an iPhone/iPod version (**$2.99**, **http://5str.us/ld8**). The iPhone 3GS and 4 models have an internal compass necessary for tracking the night sky.

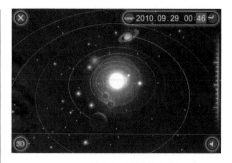

There's even a stereoscopic 3D mode, which requires inexpensive plastic-film glasses, for indoor viewing on cloudy nights.

Solar Walk

$2.99 • Vito Technology •
http://5str.us/zr4

The accurately rotating solar system in 3D at a glance

Solar Walk presents the eight planets (sorry, Pluto) in all their glory as they revolve around each other, and collectively around the sun.

The orbits are shown as lines, while the planets are outsized in relation to each other for better visibility in many views. A planet can be rotated by tapping it to bring it into full view, and then dragging.

Tap a planet or any of the major moons orbiting Mars and beyond, and then tap an i icon, and a variety of detail about the heavenly body is shown. This includes its measurements to the composition of planetary layers to the probe missions that visited it.

A rocket ship button lets you zoom in on a planet or moon after tapping it. You can rotate the orbs you're viewing, too, to see the current light and dark sides. Pinch, zooming, swiping, and dragging let you "walk" around the solar system.

As with Star Walk, you can tap a chronometer at the upper right, and use a dial to zoom through time while watching the planets move in relation to one another. This can aid in finding alignments or figuring out when a planet will be visible in the night sky.

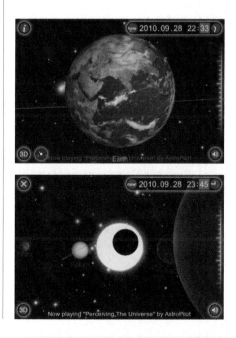

Planets ▮▯

FREE • Q Continuum • http://5str.us/hfb

An extraordinary amount of planetary data packed into a free app

The planets whirl around the Earth, and finding their current position can take an almanac, a Web site, or a trained eye. The Planets app helps you spot the other seven spheres through a few different aids, as well as view information about constellations, the sun, and Earth's moon. (Pluto is dissed in this app as in Solar Walk, p. 163.)

Views of planets are divided into several tabs. The Visibility tab is the real gem, displaying all the planets, the moon, and the sun, with their rise and set times, and whether they are visible to the unaided eye or not. A red vertical marks the current time.

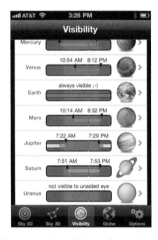

 A Sky 2D tab shows the current position of the planets and sun in a plane; during the day, only the sun is shown. A Sky 3D tab can be oriented around your view of the horizon, and shows constellations, too. You can drag to pan and pinch, and expand to see more or focus in.

If you're exceptionally geeky, a slider of labels at the top lets you see the sky via X-ray, infrared, radio, hydrogen, and microwave telescope data.

The Globes tab adds 3D, rotating low-resolution versions of the moon and eight planets, with an option to set them spinning, or pinch to zoom in.

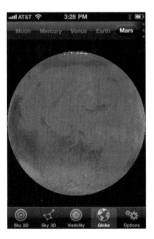

TIP: The brightest "stars" we often spot in the night sky are planets.

NASA

FREE • NASA • http://5str.us/22g

The universe of NASA missions just a tap away

NASA junkies may need to avoid this app, because it's chock full of every last bit of NASA's active missions. I can take an historic trip and review Voyager details—the Voyager 1 and 2 probes are still going, billions of miles away—or hop to the present and see yesterday's downloaded video from the Chandra X-Ray Observatory.

The main page of the app lets you search or scroll through missions. You can tap a filter button to restrict missions to specific areas of study, like the moon and Mars. Tabs for images, videos, updates, and NASA TV show the latest in all those areas.

Tap on a mission, and you dive into the specifics of that endeavor. News, images, and video are all related to the project. An alarm clock tab shows the launch date and time and duration mission duration.

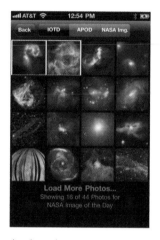

When viewing photos, you can opt to share via Facebook, Twitter, or email, or you can save the image to your Camera Roll. Videos can be shared, too.

For mission that orbit our globe, an earth icon appears at lower left on the mission page. Tap it, and you can see the satellite's track and current position.

NOTE: We're a big blue marble in space.

WeatherBug Elite

$0.99 • WeatherBug • http://5str.us/znv

Get detailed weather maps, forecasts, and webcam views

WeatherBug relies on tens of thousands of weather stations it's placed around the country to provide local weather reports and forecasts. These stations also let you see the current weather conditions through a webcam picture and an animation of several pictures from the last few hours. (Yes, it's not so useful at night, and a surprising number of cameras point at parking lots.)

The app is well designed in both of its separate iPhone/iPod touch and iPad versions, providing ready access to local weather station results, forecasts from the National Weather Service, and short videos updating current local conditions.

Although you can use WeatherBug solely to look up weather on demand, the app is most useful when you add locations. You can enter a city, state, or zip, and then add to a list you can swipe through.

For a given location, you can see current conditions, a forecast (by hour or for the next seven days), and view maps with selectable overlays of temperature, radar, and other conditions. You can also view a current video report on U.S. weather shot like a television weather segment.

WeatherBug's iPad version put all this information at a glance; the edition for the smaller screen requires a few taps.

MORE: A free version of WeatherBug Elite with ads is available for the iPhone/iPod touch (**http://5str.us/r5v**) and iPad without ads (**http://5str.us/7oi**).

AccuWeather

FREE • AccuWeather •
http://5str.us/4md

Quick glance at weather in places you define

AccuWeather presents the temperature attractively. The ad-supported free app can determine your current location to deliver weather information, and you can also enter locations you want to track.

The main display lets you swipe through multiple locations and then drill down to hourly and 15-day forecasts. The app's maps can cycle through recent precipitation radar overlays, so that you can see where rain and snow are headed.

The app includes links to the many regularly updated video reports created by AccuWeather; this includes regional reports.

The app offers weather alarms, which are local warnings of upcoming rain, snow, and other storms; and alerts, which are weather service reports for severe conditions.

 The Weather Channel Max

$3.99 • The Weather Channel •
http://5str.us/wc2

Highly focused reports on each area

The Weather Channel's app provides fine forecasting information, but it's best in two other areas: maps and video.

The Map tab lets you use location to pull up information about your current area. The i button brings up Explore Map settings which can be highly customized. You can opt for different landmarks to be shown (schools, airports, parks, and so forth) to put pins in the map that you can tap for a very local temperature. The app also lets you choose among overlay layers like 24-hour rainfall and UV Index.

Because The Weather Channel produces massive amounts of reports every day, the app provides highly localized and up-to-date video for each area you've set up to track. Tap the Video link, and the latest minute-or-so report for your area is pulled up.

MORE: AccuWeather comes in several iPhone/iPod versions. An iPad version of The Weather Channel's app is available (free, **http://5str.us/v7t**), and a free iPhone/iPod touch edition (**http://5str.us/3b4**).

18

Remote Access

The file I need is always somewhere else. The remote control is always misplaced. But we can overcome those difficulties with a variety of apps designed to give us remote access, whether it's to a media player a few feet away to files or a computer stored on the other side of the globe.

MobileMe iDisk ■■

FREE* • Apple • http://5str.us/gjh

View and share files stored in a MobileMe iDisk drive

Apple's MobileMe subscription service includes many different features useful for iOS devices including iDisk, Internet-hosted storage. You can mount iDisk like a desktop volume or use WebDAV software to access it from any platform.

The free MobileMe iDisk app provides easy access to those files from an iOS device. After logging in with your MobileMe user name and password, the iDisk file list lets you navigate among folders and select files to view. (The list is the main view on an iPhone/iPod touch, and the left pane in landscape view on an iPad.)

Either in that list, or while viewing an image or other document type supported by iOS, you can tap the Share icon and give others access to the item, with an optional expiration date and password. Tap the Shared Files icon at any time to see what's shared, make an item private, or renew an expired file.

The app also gives you access to other people's shared Public folders from their MobileMe accounts.

While you can delete files from within the app, you can't upload items. For that capability, turn to one of the other apps mentioned in this book with iDisk support built in, notably GoodReader (p. 10), and Air Sharing (p. 12).

ACCOUNT: *Requires paid MobileMe account.

Dropbox ▮▮

FREE* • Dropbox • http://5str.us/wpl

Seamless integration with a multi-platform file synchronization system

Dropbox has become a religion among some of us who manage many machines and who work with folks all over the world. The service synchronizes the contents of a folder on your desktop (Mac OS X and Windows), and can handle any number of nested folders. After you make a change to a file on one computer, the changed portions are silently and immediately sent to all other machines with which you sync. Folders can be shared with colleagues, too, making it a great tool for project collaboration.

The Dropbox app gives you access to your folders and files stored centrally by Dropbox on its servers. You can view, but not change or delete, files and folders stored in your Dropbox account; however, you can create folders and upload images and video. Like most iOS apps, Dropbox can display any text, page-layout, image, or video format that iOS supports (see p. xviii).

of temporarily cached; you can choose the size of that cache, too. You can also use the app to send links to other people to download files.

You can upload photos and videos from your device, including new pictures from its camera, if it has one. Image compression is configurable. Dropbox lets you upload full high-definition files from an iPhone 4 with the HD setting.

The app lets you view pictures in a folder as a gallery of thumbnails you can swipe through. You can mark files as favorites, which keeps them stored locally instead

The Dropbox app is free, and you can use Dropbox to store up to 2 GB of data at no cost. You must create an account at the Dropbox.com site or via the app before you can use the program.

Dropbox also works as the back-end storage for many other apps, which *can* upload and edit files stored there. The company offers a list of these at **https://www.dropbox.com/apps/list**.

ACCOUNT: *Requires a Dropbox account, which may be free or paid.

LogMeIn Ignition ▮▮

$29.99* • LogMeIn • http://5str.us/vgj

Stellar app for no-fuss remote computer access

LogMeIn Ignition is part of a family of remote-access and screen-sharing programs from company (named LogMeIn). Ignition makes your iOS device a window that peers into the screen of a desktop system on the same network or elsewhere on the Internet. The app lets you control the mouse and keyboard, as well as pinch, pan, and expand to view the remote screen.

You first set up one or more computers from the company's Web site by creating an account and downloading software to install. LogMeIn supports both Mac OS X and Windows. Each computer shows up as a named entry in a list on the site; the same appears in the app after you log in.

Tap on a computer in the list in the app, and LogMeIn creates a securely encrypted connection between the iOS device and the computer. You can move the mouse around, click, and type. A row of special icons below the screen display lets you switch between left and right mouse clicks and type special keys.

Although you can store your LogMeIn account password in Ignition, you may want to avoid this in case your device is stolen. Otherwise, a thief could gain access to your computers remotely!

Ignition is the next best thing to being there.

ACCOUNT: *Requires account with any combination of free and paid installations.

TeamViewer

FREE • TeamViewer • http://5str.us/d3i

Share desktops and presentations without prearrangement

The TeamViewer app works with desktop software for Mac OS X, Windows, and other platforms to provide remote access to a desktop. The desktop TeamViewer works as both a server and for remote access; the app is for remote access only.

You can install TeamViewer on a computer with essentially no configuration, which makes it different from LogMeIn Ignition (p. 172), which requires an account first. TeamViewer lets you set up an account to create the equivalent of buddy lists (it calls buddies "partners").

With TeamViewer active on at least one computer—with or without an account set up—you can hook in remotely.

Launch the app and you can start a session in one of two ways. In the Connect tab, enter a code number and fixed password set on the desktop software. Or you can use the Partner List, where you log into a TeamViewer account and can see and connect to machines that are part of your partner network. Your partner list includes computers you've added to your own account.

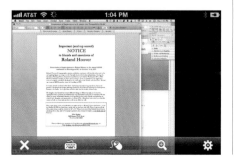

In either case, once a connection is made, the remote screen appears. As with similar apps, you have access to a virtual keyboard and mouse, as well as special function keys. Shake your device to swap between monitors if the remote device has more than one display. Pinch and expand works for controlling what you see within the frame of your device.

The company doesn't charge for this app, but that's only when you're engaged in what TeamViewer calls noncommercial use; it relies on the honor system for enforcement. Corporate licenses are quite expensive, but are priced for each active user's desktop, with no limits on many kinds of remote access.

MORE: TeamViewer Pro is $99.99 (**http://5str.us/gis**). The iPad version comes in both commercial ($139.99, **http://5str.us/a23**) and free noncommercial versions (**http://5str.us/mz1**).

iTeleport (Jaadu VNC) ██▪

$24.99 • iTeleport • http://5str.us/rd8

Access a computer remotely using standard VNC for screen sharing and data entry

iTeleport provides access to the commonly used VNC (virtual network computer) standard for remote screen, keyboard, and mouse access. VNC software is built into Mac OS X, and can be obtained at no cost or in commercial versions for nearly any computer operating system even in narrow use. That includes Mac OS X, Windows, Linux, Unix, and far more.

iTeleport takes an elegant and easy approach to making a connection. When an iOS device is on the same network as computers that use Bonjour (a mostly Apple protocol) to show their availability, the app lists them in the connection view. Other local and remote computers' settings can be entered manually.

iTeleport includes the critical option to layer encryption over its screen-sharing sessions, because VNC lacks this kind of built-in support. (iTeleport uses SSH, which is also available on nearly every platform, to create an encryption, essentially an unbreakable wrapper around your connection.)

The touchscreen on an iOS device controls the cursor on the remote machine. Standard pinch and expand gestures make the image of the remote screen smaller or larger, which is especially useful with multiple monitors. (When using Apple's Screen Sharing software, more than one monitor can be shared; with standard VNC, only the screen with the menu bar in Mac OS X can be used.)

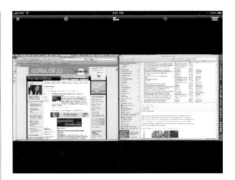

Tap in a text field that you're viewing remotely, and then tap the keyboard icon in the iTeleport overlay. Now you can type just as if you were in front of the machine.

The company behind the app, also called iTeleport, offers free Mac OS X and Windows software to enable remote access. iTeleport has a central registration system to aid connecting to computers behind firewalls or home gateways that otherwise prevent direct access. A Gmail account is used as "connective tissue" behind the scenes.

Remote

FREE • Apple • http://5str.us/qc5

Makes your mobile device into a remote control for iTunes

Remote turns iTunes into an audiovisual engine instead of a program you have to operate from a computer. In place of using a keyboard, mouse, and monitor to navigate the program, this stylish and free app lets you search, choose play-lists, and control playback. (It doesn't stream music to your iOS device.)

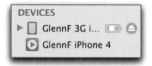

First, you pair Remote with iTunes. Launch Remote on your iOS device. Tap Settings, and you can tap Add Library. This brings up a screen showing a pass-code that needs to be entered in a copy of iTunes on the same Wi-Fi network.

On the computer you want to pair with Remote, switch to iTunes and you see a tiny Remote icon in the sidebar under Devices. Click that icon, and you can enter the code from the iOS screen. The devices are now paired. You can pair with multiple libraries, but only use one at a time.

Remote can now control playback of everything in iTunes. Items are orga-nized much like in the iPod app with categories at the bottom. Tap the More button, and tap Edit to change any of the four buttons that appear in the main screen. It's useful to promote the Search bottom to that bottom icon bar.

You can control the playback of audio and video from the app, even choosing the volume levels of audio coming out of AirPlay-connected devices (Apple TV and AirPort Express).

Leaving Remote set to remain connected in the background consumes more power than letting it disconnect, but it means that your library is always avail-able whenever you wake the device from sleep; otherwise, it has to reconnect.

TIP: If you want to play music remotely from iTunes, check out Airfoil Speakers Touch (p. 31). It works with the Airfoil desktop software to pass along audio from any program you choose on a Mac or Windows system.

AirMouse Pro ▪▪▪

$1.99 • RPA Tech • http://5str.us/bz4

Have a virtual mouse and keyboard for a computer that has a monitor

In my home, we have a Mac mini act as our video streaming, DVD, and music hub. It's plugged into an HDTV set, and sits on the top of our television cabinet in the back corner. While we can grab a keyboard and mouse and plug them in to control the mini, that's a hassle.

Instead, we turn to AirMouse Pro, an app that turns an iOS device into a combination of a touch-based trackpad and virtual keyboard.

You first install free remote access software from RPA Tech on any Mac or Windows system you want to access. The server can be password protected. Next, you launch the app and find the computer you want to control that's connected to the same local network.

Once connected, the app turns into a keyboard and trackpad. The trackpad fills half the screen in portrait mode. Shake the device or rotate it to

landscape, and the trackpad fills the whole screen. Buttons below the trackpad work as expected for left and right equivalents. Multitouch gestures, like two fingers for scrolling, work fine.

The app also includes advanced features that let you use it more like a remote control for iTunes and other programs.

MORE: A free version, Mobile Mouse Free (**http://5str.us/5d8**), is also available. It omits advanced features, like app switching, mouse acceleration, media controller, and other tools.

VLC Remote

$4.99 • Hobbyist Software • http://5str.us/49h

A nice control for those who rely on VLC

VLC is the universal video format player: free, easy to use, and open source. However, it's designed to run on a computer. If you're using that computer to put video onto a monitor or TV set to watch from a distance, it can be frustrating to manage playback.

VLC Remote pairs with VLC software using a bit of separately installed Windows or Mac software. The app lets you start, stop, and pick a playback spot, adjust volume, and manage video playlists. The app also sports controls for remotely playing DVDs on a computer.

The software lets you browse the computer's hard drive to pick files to play back. For dedicated VLC users, the app is a good counterpart.

Off Remote

$2.99 • Hobbyist Software • http://5str.us/2ed

Hit the power button rooms away

Off Remote is a switch for remotely changing the active status of a Mac OS X or Windows system; some simple software needs to be installed on the desktop server.

With Off Remote, you can be at the other end of the house and turn off a computer. Or restart it, put it to sleep, lock it, or log out of the active acount. The commands can also be set to occur after a chosen period of time.

MORE: VLC Remote comes in an iPad version ($4.99, **http://5str.us/sv1**), and a simpler iPhone/iPod touch release (**http://5str.us/htb**). Off Remote has a free version with fewer features (**http://5str.us/baf**).

19

Utilities

An iOS device is a Swiss army knife with a 1,000 empty slots ready for new tools. This chapter looks at apps that are useful for shopping, calculating, finding, waking, remembering, connecting, displaying, and more.

1Password Pro

$14.99 • Agile Web Solutions • http://5str.us/qkj

A password safe keeps your secrets available but secure

If I pick a good password, one that has a mix of letters and numbers and doesn't match words in a dictionary, how will I remember it? Better yet, why should I invent one in the first place?

1Password provides a solution to both problems. The app is a complement to desktop Mac OS X and Windows software ($39.95 for one license, $69.95 for five family members, **http://5str.us/qld**). The desktop software creates and stores passwords for logging in at a Web site. When you return to a Web site, the software can (with your permission) fill in those details for you.

The iOS app can take that data and open a Web browser sheet for Web logins, or let you copy and paste a password to

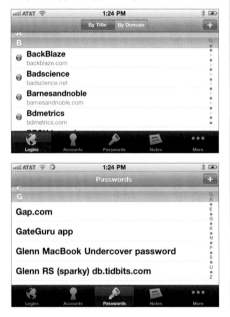

bring back to Mobile Safari or other programs for login. You can use 1Password independent of the corresponding desktop software, but it's much more difficult to capture Web logins for later use.

1Password can sync between desktop and iOS versions. A release in mid-2010 added Dropbox support, so all copies of the software write changes to the same folder, and automatically pick up new changes everywhere. Even if you don't otherwise use Dropbox, you can set up a free account (up to 2 GB of storage) to take advantage of 1Password syncing. (See p. 171 for the Dropbox app review.)

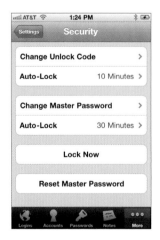

MORE: 1Password comes in three versions: Pro is designed for all three iOS devices; $9.99 iPhone/iPod touch (**http://5str.us/ka9**) and $9.99 iPad-only version (**http://5str.us/a1b**) are also available separately.

Yojimbo ██

$9.99 • Bare Bones • http://5str.us/yob

Keep your important bits and pieces close and secure while you roam

The Yojimbo app for Mac OS X is where everything I need to remember gets stuffed. It's a grab bag for text notes, PDF files, Web links, archived Web pages (downloaded and converted to a fixed page stored in the Yojimbo database), serial numbers, and images. In fact, it's harder to figure out what I don't store in the program than what I do.

Whenever I make an online purchase that has a "printer-friendly" link for the invoice or receipt, I print it straight to Yojimbo, which provides a PDF menu add-on for the print dialog box. If I buy an item with a serial number, that number heads right into the program. Any item can be secured, too, by clicking an Encrypt button.

The Yojimbo desktop program lets you tag items with as many tags as you invent. You can then create collections that are organized by tag or search filter.

Yojimbo can sync its database across multiple Mac OS X systems using a single paid MobileMe account. But there had never been an easy or secure way to take that data with you on the go.

This app fills the gap. It automatically syncs with Yojimbo 3.0 whenever the program is fired up on the same Wi-Fi network. You can also tap a refresh button in the item browsing tab at any time.

The library, collections, and other data come right over to the app for access. Encrypted items are unlocked using the same password you set in the desktop

software. (I never store my password for Yojimbo in the Mac OS X or iOS keychain, as that would defeat the purpose of encryption if my machine were accessed or stolen while I was logged in.)

Because I'm a dedicated Yojimbo user, I'm willing to overlook the missing ability in 1.0 to create items and modify tags. The utility of having all that information I store on my desktop at my mobile disposal outweighs (for the moment) the lack of controls to modify or add to it.

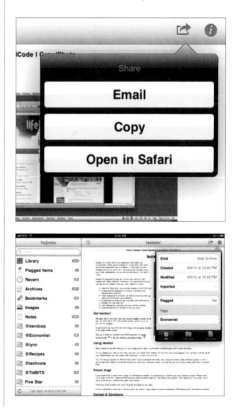

Dragon Dictation ■■

FREE • Nuance Communications • http://5str.us/f5r

Speak and have the app turn your words into text

Dragon NaturallySpeaking and Dragon Dictate are the best speech-recognition software ever developed, and they constantly improve. However, mobile devices don't have enough processing power to turn audio into text with the necessary level of accuracy. That's where this free adjunct app from Nuance steps in. It takes what you say into a microphone (a headset may be better), and transmits the audio to Nuance's servers for conversion.

The quality of conversion is fairly good, although corrections are often necessary. This isn't onerous if the majority of what you speak is correctly recognized. You can opt to delete entire words, or tap the keyboard icon and use full letter-by-letter editing. The app supports up to 60 seconds of recording at a time, but you can restart dictating indefinitely after each minute. Nuance recommends recording a few sentences at a time.

The app supports a number of punctuation marks and special characters, although these are unfortunately not documented in the app itself. (See **http://5str.us/6fd**, and click Features and Usage at left.) You can also allow the program to upload all your contacts' names, which improves recognition for those people when you speak their names as part of your dictation.

Once you have your recognized text, you can pass it on via a text message, email, Facebook, or Twitter, or copy it to for use in another app.

Why is this marvelous app free? Nuance gets access to an enormous variety of spoken words (anonymously captured) to improve its expensive desktop software, as *New York Times* columnist David Pogue explained at **http://nyti.ms/cweSPn**. The app also acts as an ad for Nuance's desktop software.

MORE: Dragon NaturallySpeaking for Windows starts at $199.99 (**http://5str.us/vyc**) and Dragon Dictate for Mac OS X starts at $179.99 (**http://5str.us/22j**)

Amazon Mobile ▪▪▪

FREE • Amazon.com • http://5str.us/kck

A portable portal into the ecommerce giant paired with uncanny photo recognition

Amazon Mobile demonstrates the power of mobile devices by providing an easier way to find, order, and track goods than on a full-sized computer's Web browser.

The app lets you search, of course, after which you can drill down into the results to view reviews, editorial descriptions, pictures, and other associated information for a given item. You can see all available product conditions (new and used) for books and media.

If you sign in to an existing Amazon.com account (or create one), your 1-Click purchase settings are available. You can also add items to a cart and review the contents of that cart by clicking a button. The app can place the order, too. Terrific, right?

But that's not what makes this app more interesting than Amazon's Web site. The Remembers tab is the key; a built-in camera is required. Tap the camera icon and take a picture of an item you want

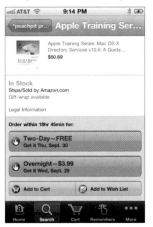

to purchase from Amazon. That could be a book cover, a physical object like a clock, a toy, or what have you. Tap Use.

The picture is uploaded so you can jog your own memory later. But the eerie part is the photo is also sent to some combination of computer and human analysis to figure out whether there's a matching or close item.

I snapped a shot of a 30-year-old children's book cover (no bar code), and it was matched in a matter of seconds. A picture of a large clock hanging on my wall was also matched nearly instantly.

The danger with this app is that it makes compare prices too easy: you can check constantly while on the go—and wind up with piles of Amazon boxes waiting on your porch.

TIP: To avoid immediate gratification, you can place items in the app's shopping cart to review later. The app also lets you add items to and review wishlists.

Find My iPhone

FREE* • Apple • http://5str.us/fcf

Keep track of your iOS device when it's lost or taken away

Your phone is missing. Or your iPad. And you know you had it just a minute ago. Or , worse, someone snatches it out of your hand. Where can it be? Find My iPhone (despite its limiting name) will help you track down any iOS device that has a current network connection, as well as one that connects at some point after you first attempt to find it.

First, the requirements: you need a MobileMe account ($100 to $150 per year) to enable Find My iPhone.

Second, the service only works when either Push or Fetch (or both) synchronization is turned on (Settings > Mail, Contacts, Calendar > Fetch New Data). (Push is used to send new data your iOS device whenever it's available; Fetch retrieves email and other information on a regular schedule.)

Third, you must activate the service for each device you own (Settings > Mail, Contacts, Calendar > your MobileMe account > Find My iPhone).

Fourth, a device can only report its position when it is connected to a network.

That said, the service and this app are invaluable. The app lets you quickly see the last-known position of the device. On Apple mobile gear that has Push enabled, Find My iPhone can query for

the current position. Precision is GPS exact for an iPhone or a 3G iPad; less accurate Wi-Fi positioning is used for the iPod touch and Wi-Fi-only iPad model.

Launch the app and log in to MobileMe, and a list of your active devices with the service turned on are shown. It can take up to a few minutes to retrieve the current location of each, even if they're all online.

Whether or not your missing iOS device is connected, you can send a command to carry out one of three actions through the app: trigger a loud sound regardless of whether the device's audio is muted with an optional message; turn on a PIN code for access, which immediately knocks the device into a locked state; or wipe the hardware clean.

ACCOUNT: *Find My iPhone requires a paid MobileMe account. The account details must be entered on each device you want to track with the Find My iPhone/iPad/iPod touch service, and that service must be set to be active.

That last choice is the nuclear option. As long as you've recently connected your iOS device to iTunes, you will have a backup of your apps, preferences, mail, and other data. Wiping it remotely only destroys any data created that you didn't sync remotely. (New contacts or modified calendar events, for instance, will be synced via MobileMe if you have that over-the-air feature activated.)

Wiping can take a minute or so on any iOS device released in 2009 or later; 2007 and 2008 hardware lacks an encryption chip that makes erasing a device a simple matter, and can take hours to remove your data.

If a device isn't connected to a network or is powered down, the next time it accesses a cellular or Wi-Fi network the device responds to whatever commands were sent.

Of course, if your device is lost or stolen, an app seemingly has no use, right? You can access Find My iPhone from any Web browser, but this free, small app can be installed on another iOS device (perhaps that of a friend), and your MobileMe username and password are all you'll need to access it—and your password isn't stored when you're done.

TIP: MobileMe subscriptions are cheaper when purchased from online retailers, often 20 to 30 percent less than from Apple. Look at Amazon.com and others for a boxed serial number for a new subscription or a renewal.

TextExpander ▌▪

$4.99 • Smile Software • http://5str.us/6u6

Shortcuts expand to avoid tedious retyping in many writing and posting apps

TextExpander turns shortcuts into longer text—as simple as that. It's a subset of what used to be called a "macro" program, an old word-processing term. Figure out text that you're going to enter over and over again, like the current date, your name, your address, or even a common phrase (like "Sincerely yours"). Enter that, and then an associated shortcut (like "SY").

TextExpander includes a scratchpad where you can write and use its shortcut expansions, and then copy or forward elsewhere. But it's most useful within a few dozen writing apps that directly support TextExpander and its shortcuts.

You can then type your shortcut in those apps and the text is magically replaced.

The developer keeps a list at **http://5str. us/ud6**. Apps with TextExpander support in this book include Twitter (p. 22), Elements (p. 158), and Simplenote (p. 133).

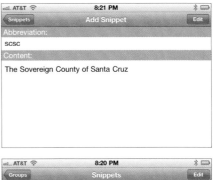

TIP: You can use special placeholders to automatically insert the date, year, or other items. A full list can be found in the desktop software's FAQ at **http://5str.us/hjr**.

AT&T myWireless Mobile

FREE • AT&T • http://5str.us/499

A one-stop shop for AT&T account information and service changes

Whether or not you enjoy being an AT&T customer, there's no question you'll like its iPhone account app. myWireless Mobile consolidates all your account-related information in one place and lets you make service changes. It simplifies information retrieval that requires more effort on the company's Web site.

With AT&T's limited cellular data plans, myWireless is an easy way to check on current usage to see how close you are to exhausting the current billing cycle's data plan. Tap Usage, then the Data tab.

The Features option is also useful whenever you need to modify your subscription services. For instance, when I want to enable AT&T Navigator, I can tap Features, select my number, scroll to AT&T Navigator for iPhone, and tap to turn on the service. (A separate free download of the navigation app is required.)

The app can manage multiple lines in a family plan, as well as single-line accounts.

Mark the Spot

FREE • AT&T Services • http://5str.us/usz

Give AT&T feedback on the spot

AT&T has received plenty of criticism as the exclusive iPhone seller and network in the U.S. (at this writing). Mark the Spot is supposed to help deflect some of that criticism and improve the network.

If a call fails or you have another network problem, launch the app, make sure the map shows where you are, and choose the problem: Failed Call Attempt, No Coverage, and so forth. If you don't have a live data connection, the report is sent later.

TIP: AT&T's tethering option for the iPhone at $45 per month ($25 for data plus a $20 tethering fee) is more expensive than Virgin Mobile's on-demand, unlimited $40 service with a MiFi portable router (**http://5str.us/qng**).

Night Stand HD

$4.99 • Spoonjuice • http://5str.us/lrh

Miss your old-style alarm clock? Here's a replacement

Just another five minutes. Please. Just another five minutes.

All right, I'll get up if I have to, especially when facing the beautifully designed and nostalgia-inducing alarm clock faces offered by Night Stand HD. The app simulates an old-fashioned alarm clock, with a choice of what you see.

You can add multiple alarms, pairing a sound to each or a song from your iPod library. (In a bit of whimsy, one of the included alarm "tones" is Scream, a terrifying high-pitched yell with an echo. I'll pass, thanks.) Alarms can go off once, or be set to repeat on any combination of days of the week.

If you've set music to play when you wake up, you can also choose how long it plays. The app lets you choose a location (or automatically finds one) to show current weather details, too.

A hilarious option for turning off your alarm requires that you wake up a little. You have to solve a multiple-choice math equation to still the clock!

MORE: A universal free version is also available (**http://5str.us/9k5**) with fewer clock designs, alarms, and other features.

Air Display ▌▌

$9.99 • Avatron Software • http://5str.us/1o1

Need another monitor and don't have the table space or funds? Tap an app

Why not extend your desktop to the screen of your iOS device? Air Display makes it happen. The clever app fools your computer into thinking an iPhone, iPod touch, or iPad is just another monitor. You install a software package onto your computer (Mac OS X on Intel system, or most versions of Windows XP, Vista, or 7), restart, and then launch Air Display in iOS. Both the computer and the iOS device have to be on the same Wi-Fi network for the extension to work.

Air Display now actds just like another monitor attached to your computer (see figure at upper right). Tap on the iPad or other device to control the cursor or you can use the computer's mouse.

iOS devices can't update a screen very quickly compared to a standard LCD montior. That, coupled with network bandwidth limits, make Air Display slower than your main monitor or monitors. It's best to put items that aren't animated on the virtual screen, such as palettes from a layout program, text-based software, or a Twitter client.

Air Display is probably best used with a laptop on the road, where you want some extra territory and aren't trooping around with an LCD panel. Or if you're just tired of Photoshop CS5's floating palettes taking up nearly an entire monitor's worth of space.

TIP: Use the Arrangement tab in Mac OS X's Display dialog box to put the Air Display monitor in the right location relative to your existing monitor(s).

Easy Wi-Fi ▪▫

FREE • Devicescape • http://5str.us/3s9

Connect to Wi-Fi hotspots without constantly re-entering passwords

Devicescape specializes in connecting Wi-Fi devices to Wi-Fi hotspots without you needing to lift more than perhaps one finger. The Easy Wi-Fi app combines three different functions in a single place: accounts, connections, and maps.

Easy Wi-Fi doesn't sell Wi-Fi access, but, through its Web site or the app, you can enter your login details for any of hundreds of for-fee or login-required networks. For instance, AT&T DSL and fiber (U-Verse) and Qwest subscribers receive free Wi-Fi access accounts as part of their broadband service. And, if you use Boingo Wireless's laptop service (not Boingo Mobile, see p. 191), you can link in that account, too.

At a hot spot, you have to launch the app the first time you visit due to restrictions Apple places on its operating system that prevent direct access to network settings by developers. On subsequent occasions, no launch should be required. A big friendly set of green Wi-Fi signal waves indicates when you're connected, along with other details as needed.

The app can show hotspot details on a map either by using your current location or letting you perform a search on an address.

Pins mark known hotspots, whether commercial or public. Blue pins indicate free access, while red pins show locations that require a fee, account, or code. The number of waves emanating from the pin indicates network quality.

Tap a pin, and you can get more information about the location if it's available, such as a rating, or add details.

Assuming you want to do something after connecting, Easy Wi-Fi includes an app launcher; tap the red button at upper left. You can customize what's in the list from a small set of choices.

TIP: A 99¢ in-app option removes ads for three months.

Boingo Mobile ▮▮

FREE* • Boingo Wireless • http://5str.us/45r

Connect with a click at 125,000 Wi-Fi hotspots

Boingo Mobile extends the usefulness of any iOS device. While carriers in the U.S. and several other countries include in iPhone service plans modest to completely unlimited use of Wi-Fi hotspots, those offers don't include all paid locations in a given country or region.

If you own an iPod touch or iPad (the Wi-Fi only model or a 3G unit without an active cellular data plan), you need a Wi-Fi network connection to access the Internet at all. If you're as frugal as I am, you'd also rather not pay extra for Wi-Fi, or at least not pay for each connection you make. (On a typical trip for me, that could be airport, airport, coffeeshop, hotel, airport, airport.)

The $7.95-per-month Boingo Mobile subscription ties an iOS device into 125,000 locations worldwide. The service works with any iOS device (with 3G active or not). In the US, Boingo connects with tens of thousands of hotspots.

It's a way to avoid excess data charges on cellular data networks, such as AT&T. Paying $7.95 per month instead of $10 or more each time you cross a monthly limit may be a good tradeoff.

Apple doesn't allow any app to touch network settings directly, so when you arrive at a hotspot you first join the network, and then launch the Boingo Mobile app. If it's a Boingo-affiliated hotspot a Connect button appears. Tap it, and you're connected.

Boingo Mobile also includes a hotspot map that can use your current location. Tap a map pin, and the name and address for the selected location are shown with a link for driving directions.

Boingo also offers Boingo Wi-Fi Credits (**http://5str.us/wwp**), an app that lets you buy one-hour credits at $1.99 each (or 11 for $19.99) for its worldwide locations using your iTunes Account. The first hour is free.

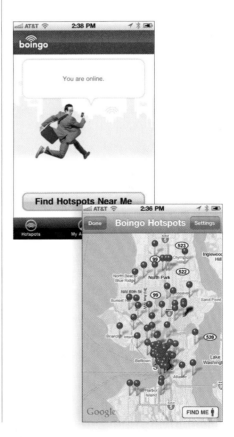

ACCOUNT: *Requires an account for hotspot access. You can purchase a single session pass or a recurring subscription.

PCalc RPN Calculator ▮▯▮

$9.99 • TLA Systems • http://5str.us/54t

You'd think a calculator would be boring. It isn't

C'mon! $9.99 for a calculator app? Really?

Yes. And it's worth it if you regularly need the paper tape, engineering, programming, or scientific functions built in. PCalc even includes Reverse Polish Notation (RPN) for those who cut their teeth on 1970s HP calculators.

As a basic calculator, the app is tops. You can opt for different default layouts in portrait or landscape, such as the plain Default for one and Engineering for another. You can pick "skins" or color themes as well (those apply to both orientations).

To undo a calculation, swipe left on the results area; do so repeatedly to step back further and further. Swipe down on the display area, and you reveal more information, including the current contents of memory. Tap the i, swipe down,

and tap Advanced Settings, and you can choose what the extra fields contain.

But you can dive much deeper than just straightforward calculations. Specially labeled keys bring up more information. The **42** button, a tip of the hat to Douglas Adams, dislays a list of constants sorted by type, like atomic and mathematical.

Tap the **A→B** button, and a host of conversions becomes available. You can use routine calculations, such as energy, legnth, and weight.

But PCalc also includes currency conversion, with an automatic update if the numbers haven't been refreshed recently. You can tap Update Currency Rates to force an update, too. The conversion area lets you scroll through widely used currencies first, and then move on to less-common ones.

The app generates a "paper tape" of calculations that you can email or copy.

MORE: A free version of PCalc (universal, **http://5str.us/168**) omits advanced modes, which can be added through individual in-app purchases.

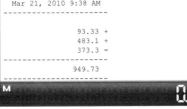

Operators, like plus and multiply by, are shown as part of a sequence below the running total. Swipe down, and you can see a virtual tape of the transactions, which you can email.

Swipe on the main button area to the right, and advanced mathematical operators appear for handling sines, cosines, square, logarithms, and more.

If you're calculating money, tap the i button at the lower right, and turn on Round for Currency. This will display the currency symbol for your current locale, and round fractions to two decimal places.

Calcbot

$1.99 • Tapbots •
http://5str.us/r73

A replacement for Calculator when you don't need all the oomph of Pcalc

Calcbot is a attractive replacement for the Apple-provided Calculator app. The main screen offers the usual suspects (zero through nine, I m watching you), but once you start entering a calculation, the difference is apparent.

Calvetica

$2.99 • Wesley Taylor Design • http://5str.us/vmi

Attractive presentation of calendar data with clever ways to view and modify events

Calvetica isn't for everyone, but if you love an austere interface and the Helvetica typeface, you'll love this app. Calvetica is a replacement for iOS's built-in Calendar app. Events added or changed in this app, iCal or BusyCal on a Mac, the Calendar app, or MobileMe all synchronize together.

Calvetica makes a bold statement from its home screen: a large year, a set of months, and a calendar grid with dots next to dates to indicate how many events occur on those dates. Tap the date, and the day view appears. Tap line icons at the bottom to show events, a range of hours you set, or all hours.

You can create a new event just by tapping the blank line next to an hour. If you want to create an event for an hour start that's already filled, or you want to start at 15-minute intervals, a red popout menu appears with :00, :15, :30, and :45. Tap a number, and fill in the event.

To edit an event, tap it. To set an alarm or change it, tap the alarm icon to the event's right. Alarms are shown in black if inactive, and red if a time is set. Swipe across an event that's not being edited, and you can tap a cross of arrows to move the event's time, a magnifying glass to set details like duration, and a checkbox to choose the calendar to which the event belongs.

Calvetica picks up several Swiss themes: Helvetica is a Swiss face (one that's long battled for Swiss dominance with Univers) that's had a movie made about it; the red of the Swiss flag is used in the app, plus its square cross appears in the app's icon.

Having studied for years in my youth with Swiss and Swiss-trained designers, I'd say Calvetica gets the aesthetic mostly right—but my teachers would have said too many different sizes of type were in use.

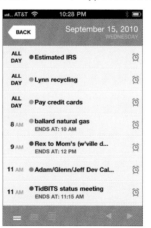
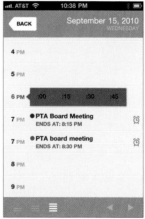

Flashlight+

$0.99* • More Blu Sky • http://5str.us/nrd

A button, a strobe, and sending out an SOS

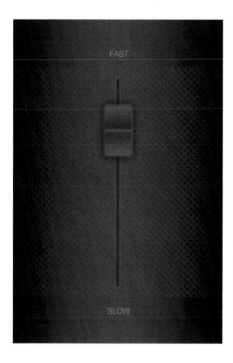

There are a million (not literally) flashlight apps available from the App Store which light up an iOS device's screen in shades, strobes, and other effects. Nifty. But Flashlight+, which works only with an iPhone 4, uses the LED flash in the back, which is far brighter. The app has simple controls: a big button for on and off, an option to strobe the light, and a screen to flash an SOS.

✳Flashlight✳

FREE* • Henri Asseily • http://5str.us/49b

Single-screen control of an iPhone 4's LED light

This free app uses a single screen to control the iPhone 4's LED flash. You can turn the light on and off, set the strobe, and tap to flash a light—what the app calls Manual Control.

HARDWARE: *Requires an iPhone 4.

CardStar ▇▪

FREE • Mesa Dynamics • http://5str.us/wh8

Consolidate your barcoded membership cards into an app

Open your wallet or pocketbook, and see how many cards you carry that bear a barcode instead of a magnetic strip. That many, huh? Shouldn't a computer be able to free you from the tedium of carrying computer-readable codes? CardStar can.

The app can't (yet) scan your barcodes directly, sad to say, but the free app has dozens of preset entries for department and grocery stores, membership clubs, libraries, museums, and other businesses and institutions built in.

To add cards, you tap the + and select the business or group type or All Merchants. (Merchants, confusingly, includes public institutions like libraries, and membership clubs, like gyms). You can select from a list of all included firms or organizations, or type in a search. (The program's makers say you can email them with missing categories and they'll add them in an update.)

Tap Done after selecting the right company or group, and then tap the field beneath Enter Membership Number. Tap in the number, and you're done. From the main view, tap the name, and the barcode appears, ready for scanning whenever you'd normally show your physical card.

Mesa Dynamics notes that some newer scanners cannot read barcodes from the Retina Display screen used with the iPhone 4 and 4th-generation iPod touch. However, the app shows the barcode's number, which can be entered by hand. The firm is working on the solution.

CardStar provides associated information where available in the Info tab, such as a link to a store locator or customer service contacts usually launching Mobile Safari. In a future update, the app's maker plans to include coupons alongside particular brands for which you have affinity cards.

TIP: Looking for apps that scan barcodes, too? See Amazon.com Mobile (p. 183), Microsoft's Bing (p. 137), QuickMark 4 (p. 142) , and RedLaser (p. 143).

Index

Work and Play with Your iPad Today!

Plan a vacation, create a recipe scrapbook or get productive with Pages, Keynote, and Numbers. No matter what you want to do with your iPad, Peachpit has a book to help. Become an iPad whiz in no time!

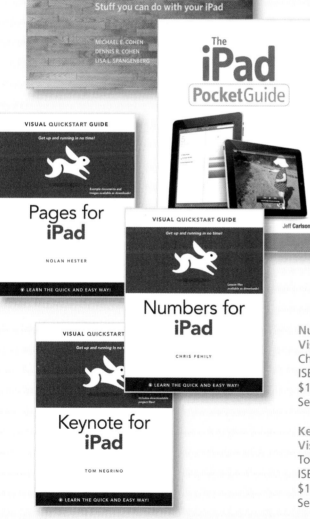